A LIFE

INTERRUPTED

THE STORY OF MY BATTLE WITH BULLYING AND
OBSESSIVE-COMPULSIVE DISORDER

SUMI MUKHERJEE

MOUNTAIN SPRINGS HOUSE
INDIANAPOLIS

Editing: Lee Porche
Print Formatting: Lynn Hubbard

DEDICATION

This book is dedicated to all people around the world who are working hard to overcome bullying and mental illness.

Honest, compelling and at times unnerving, Life Interrupted keeps you both interested and entertained. Sumi did an incredible job of sharing the raw truth about growing up as a bullied individual while tying in the OCD connection. It is an easy to read book which can clearly be understood by anyone who works with individuals living with OCD. I have a clearer idea of what these children live with on a day in and day out basis now that I have read Sumi's book. I once had a very narrow view of OCD. That view has been expanded. The book has given me insight on how to work better with Youth in Crisis.

Sumi's explanation of the life challenges he went through growing up being bullied doesn't make a person feel sorry for him, but proud of him. I've worked individually with Sumi to bring his story to the Minnesota School System. He is opening the gateway for the suffering to stop. Thousands of conversations are now being started by children who have been bullied. They may never have had the opportunity to share their thoughts and feelings about being bullied if they had not read his book or heard him speak.

My recommendation is to read Life Interrupted, share it and talk about it.

Denise Colby-Youth Counselor, Minneapolis, MN

This is a brave experiential account. The author of this short book is a courageous young man, a second generation immigrant from India, who was born in Canada, came to the US at 9 months of age, and knew this country as his only country. Sumi Mukherjee, age 34, is remarkably honest and direct in identifying his experience with bullying, anxiety, depression, and Obsessive Compulsive Disorder. He has little self-pity or whining tones and seems remarkably mentally healthy beyond his "casebook" diagnosis of obsessive compulsive disorder (OCD) which was exacerbated with the trauma of persistent long-term bullying.

The fact that the author, as a teenager, was able to keep the secret of his OCD from age 16 until 21 from his involved and loving parents (both well educated and one a PhD psychologist), speaks to the peer isolation, stigma, shame and fear under whose shadows he had to live. Concerned as to why he was treated this way, Sumi sneaked into his mother's psychological books, and thought that he might have schizophrenia. The fear of further isolation through hospitalization / confinement to 'homes for the crazy' was another factor. Finally at the age of 21, purely out of desperation, he was able to tell his father how he was suffering.

Indeed, the author's experience of being wounded by bullying holds a prominent place in the story. The OCD took hold at age 16 while the trauma of bullying were ongoing. The OCD trafficked on Sumi's images of bullies and he began to believe he had to perform compulsive behaviors to protect those he loved such as family members. His stark details of his thoughts and frenzied attempts to circumvent them are refreshing. Such honesty on this subject has been beyond my experience and mindboggling about the intensity of loss of control and suffering both in bullying and OCD. It makes the story very real and impactful.

This young man's healing journey is, of course, not straight-line progressive. Sumi finally gets some help, but then rebels. As a high school graduate, he wants to experiment with who he is and goes off his medications and experiments with alcohol. This choice is one many of us working with young people and mental illness have witnessed.

The depth of Sumi's learning about OCD itself is huge. The level at which an OCD sufferer has to engage / commit to actually make a difference beyond his own benefit and the 'the prescription drugs-only' choice is a profound learning for Sumi. He has obviously had excellent help from his family, his therapists, psychiatrists, and a very brief residential treatment, during which he finally (1) got the right medication prescription for him and (2) that OCD was even worse in its control on some others. However, to make needed changes, Sumi still had to learn and institute the cognitive behavioral skills necessary. This process of learning took many years out of his life, depriving him of social life and other opportunities as he was able to perform at a minimal level compared to his potential. This reviewer bases this assumption on the clarity of his writing which indicates a person of exceptional self-awareness, intelligence and strength. After being in control of the OCD, Sumi next had to also deal with the real "rocky road" of the impact of the social-emotional 'lost years' ! A Life Interrupted is an apt title for this book.

The most poignant part of the book is when the author, Sumi, as an adult, sets up a meeting with the man who bullied him the most intensely during his childhood. That episode was resolved in an understanding and freedom/emancipation which reinforced Sumi's payoff for taking this courageous step of confronting one of his oppressors. The transformation of the bully in a much weaker person in adulthood as compared to the childhood bully, had its impact. Unfortunately, a few years later Sumi accidentally read this man's obituary in the paper and learned that he had had schizophrenia, the very illness of which Sumi had been so afraid!

A Life Interrupted is a quick read. It is like a peanut, small but full of meat. It includes tips for OCD sufferers, their parents, significant others and also gives encouragement that even in its severe forms, OCD can be managed sufficiently to render an individual functional. It would be appropriate for anyone afflicted with OCD or bullying or depression/anxiety/PTSD. All physicians should read it. All psychologists in training and in practice should read it. All psychotherapists should read it. All teachers and professors should read it. Its experiential value and flavor grounds the reader in the milieu of a cruel combination of bullying, anxiety OCD, depression.

I felt somewhat cheated after learning so intimately about the author's distress that I didn't know more about Sumi's successes and his whole self, by the time I was finished reading. He is much more than his vulnerability due to OCD and seems worth-knowing. Perhaps his next book will include more of the whole mix of what makes Sumi a person of interest.

By Gail Anderson, MA, LP
Published in the MPA (Minnesota Psychological Association) Journal
Published in the MWP (Minnesota Women in Psychology) Newsletter

This delightful little autobiography is written in a simple, concise style that engages the reader in the journey through the harrowing hell of obsessive compulsive disorder. Of significance is the pain involved in being misdiagnosed, bullied and ostracized by peers. It is interesting how in spite of having a mother who is a psychologist, Mukherjee's problem remained undiscovered until later in life as a young adult. Unfortunately, as a young child, he was privy to his mother's psychological literature which served to confound the issue as he then became convinced that he was a paranoid schizophrenic. Ironically, one of his worst bullies later suicided from that disorder but only after Sumi was able to confront him and deal with his inner fears. Several important themes are raised in this book. Perhaps the most important one is how easy it is for the disorder or illness to be misdiagnosed by clinicians as in the painful case of Sumi. He appears to be suffering from Post Traumatic Stress Disorder, low self esteem, depression, anxiety, perfectionistic traits, academic failure and an inability to focus. One of the most compelling arguments the writer makes is the necessity for an accurate diagnosis so that the psychopharmacological aspects of the illness can be appropriately treated as was the case with Sumi, but only after a painful struggle over twenty years. Themes of shame, guilt, racism and inadequacy are painfully portrayed as we relive Sumi's experiences in early childhood and puberty. It is only as a young adult that he is able to engage in a heterosexual relationship of significance. The multifaceted aspects of the illness are graphically depicted through Sumi's eyes. This book should be in every clinician's library. It is a useful therapeutic adjunct and would be of value to school counselors as well as the general public.

Joan Neehall, Ph.D is a Registered Psychologist in private practice in Edmonton, Alberta. She is a fellow of the American Board of Forensic Examiners.

In this raw, emotional book, Sumi Mukherjee details his life with OCD, anxiety and depression. The impact of living with these illnesses, which in fact were triggered by the extreme bullying that he endured for many years, affected every aspect of his life. Sumi's honest account of his struggles is heartbreaking, but as he gets older his inner strength shines through and he learns to cope and fight for a successful happy life as an adult. He shares his experiences with therapy, medications and an OCD treatment program. He also emphasizes how important the continued love and support of his parents has been throughout his life. He has an optimism that is encouraging to all. This is a powerful story that lets people know they are not alone in their struggles.

By Wendy Chase, a parent

There are many books now available on obsessive compulsive disorder, but few give an uncensored description of what it is actually like to live with shocking, unwanted obsessions. *A Life Interrupted-The Story of my Battle with Bullying and Obsessive Compulsive Disorder* gives readers an insider's view of the devastating impact OCD and bullying can have on a person's life. He also shares his path to standing up to his childhood bully and OCD, which takes much courage and flexibility. The reward is insight, change, and the feeling of being back in control. The author is genuine in his description of his OCD symptoms and his successes and challenges along the way. It is well written and the author is even able to interject some humor into sharing his story. While the descriptions of the OCD thoughts are graphic, they are not uncommon and many people will be able to relate to this book.

Renae M. Reinardy, Psy.D.
Licensed Psychologist
Founder, Lakeside Center for Behavioral Change (Minnetonka, MN and Fargo, ND)

For more comments/reviews visit www.bullyingandocd.com

TABLE OF CONTENTS

INTRODUCTION

To every underdog, underachiever, and late bloomer out there who never quite discovered his or her true potential in life... as of yet, this book is for you. This book is also on behalf of everyone around the globe who has committed suicide as a result of being bullied; suffered anxiety, depression, and a loss of self-esteem as a result of being bullied; and for those who are currently enduring harassment and/or a mental illness today. Please know that I really do understand what you're feeling and living with on a daily basis. To the loved ones of those bullying victims who killed themselves, I could have very well ended up with the same exact fate as the dear person you lost. I promise you, I will continue to do positive things and keep your loved ones alive through my positive actions. If my book can help even one person be a little stronger, keep the faith a little more alive, or grow even a tiny bit wiser in how he/she deals with his or her personal struggle, than my personal decades of struggling were not all lost or in vain.

In spite of everything that has happened to me for almost two decades, I feel lucky today that I am able to write about my battle with Bullying and Obsessive-Compulsive Disorder. But in order to do so, I have had to accept the possibility that no one may care to hear my story. After all, I'm not a doctor or a professor with a degree in psychology. I'm also not a celebrity or well-known public figure with the power, charisma, and ability needed to draw and dazzle thousands of readers.

Far from it, in fact. I am just an ordinary person whose life has been consumed with extraordinary pain and hardship; a terrified child and young man forced to carry a burden more tremendous and taxing than words can describe. As a now educated sufferer, I know there are many of you out there who carry a similar burden. Yours may come in the form of your own affliction, or through loving someone dearly who has been bullied and/or who has OCD. You may even be unsure if this diagnosis applies to you. In any case, I hope I am able to reach out to all whose lives have been touched by bullying and anxiety related illness. If one person were to read any part of this book and get something positive from it, then I'll know I have made a difference beyond finding inner peace for myself.

Throughout my life it has always been very therapeutic for me to write, especially concerning a subject that I am passionate about. But writing about this ordeal has felt overwhelming, as it is difficult to reflect on so many traumatic events and relive the horrors, which I can barely believe I was able to somehow survive. I'm afraid of unlocking the door, to indescribably disturbing memories, as though recalling the worst of what happened can somehow make it happen all over again. But that right there is the seductive nature of this fascinating disease. Therefore, I feel writing can only help in my quest to heal and understand. So here it is. This is the true, graphic account of a life interrupted: it is the story of my battle with bullying and obsessive-compulsive disorder.

> Out of the night that covers me,
> Black as the Pit from pole to pole,
> I thank whatever gods may be
> For my unconquerable soul.
>
> In the fell clutch of circumstance
> I have not winced nor cried aloud.
> Under the bludgeonings of chance
> My head is bloody, but unbowed.
>
> Beyond this place of wrath and tears
> Looms but the Horror of the shade,
> And yet the menace of the years
> Finds, and shall find, me unafraid.
>
> It matters not how strait the gate,
> How charged with punishments the scroll,
> I am the master of my fate:
> I am the captain of my soul.
> "INVICTUS" - WILLIAM ERNEST HENLEY

ACKNOWLEDGEMENTS

There are many people I would like to thank and recognize as having had a role in the successful publication of this book.

First and foremost, on a personal level, I would not have survived or accomplished any of this without the unrelenting support of my immediate family over the course of my lifetime; that being Bimal Mukherjee, Asha Mukherjee, Sonil Mukherjee, and Gussy Mukherjee (our late beloved dog).

I also would like to thank all other loved ones and friends whose presence over the years has helped me to reach my potential and to now try to help others. Among these, I would like to extend a very special thanks to Mr. Lance Jameson of Port Aransas, TX, for introducing me to the wonderful people at Mountain Springs House Publishing in Indiana.

My sincere thanks also go to the following four professional psychologists for their detailed reviews of this book, identifying the value of the book for professionals such as teachers, school administrators, counselors, school social workers, school psychologists, and all other mental health professionals, as well as for OCD patients and their loved ones, parents of students of all ages, and the general public: Gail Anderson, M.A., LP, Professional Psychologist, Monticello, MN; Joan Neehall, Ph.D, Registered Psychologist in private practice in Edmonton, AB, Canada; Dr. Renae Reinardy, Ph.D, Psychologist, Founder of the Lakeside Center for Behavioral Change in Minnetonka, MN, and Fargo, ND (also co-founder of OCD Twin Cities); Irene Tobis, PhD., Director, OCD Brief Intensive Treatment Program, Anxiety Treatment Center of Austin, and OCD Texas President in Austin, TX.

I would also like to thank the following people for their invaluable support of this book and for their assistance in developing opportunities for spreading the most critical message in this book regarding impact of bullying on mental health: Andrew Fefer of Eau Claire, WI; Sean Herstein, Teacher at Milken Community High School in Los Angeles, CA; Jenina Rothstein, Teacher at Buffalo-

Hanover-Montrose Schools in Buffalo, MN; Candace Whittaker, Family & Community Empowerment (FCE) Specialist at Northwest Suburban Integration School District in Brooklyn Center, MN; Barb Janski, Diversity & Curriculum Integration Coordinator at Buffalo-Hanover-Montrose Schools in Buffalo, MN; Peggy Palumbo, Health Teacher at Crosswinds Arts & Science School in Woodbury, MN.

My sincere thanks also go to Sonia Miller-Van Oort, Attorney & Founder at Sapientia Law Group in Minneapolis, MN, for her professional support for this book.

Finally, I would also like to thank the Staff at Rogers Memorial Hospital in Oconomowoc, WI, for their excellent OCD treatment program which helped me reclaim my life from this devastating illness.

CHAPTER ONE
A HAPPY KID GROWING UP

Over time it has become clear to me that a person's greatest privilege in life, regardless of what it may be, is often the thing they will take most for granted. Being human, we can get lost longing for what we don't have - aching for that which we feel is still missing - and lose sight of the miracles staring us in the face on a daily basis. For me in my life, my greatest blessing, privilege and miracle is, and has always been, my family. They are an essential part of who I am as a person, how my OCD symptoms played out, and why I feel so incredibly lucky to be who I am today.

I was a very happy kid growing up, and quite mobile for my age as well. Within the first few years of my life I had already done quite a bit of traveling. I was born in Calgary, Alberta, Canada, spent two years living in Florida, and then moved to Minnesota, where I was raised and still live to this day, in spite of the bitter cold winters and mosquitoes in the summer. Mom and dad were both born and raised in different parts of India, but met one another by chance in Calgary, where mom had a job and dad was in school.

As is the case with many couples, they didn't exactly hit it off smoothly at first, but there the blame lies solely with my father. While working at a movie theatre with a student group on an uneventful evening, he met my mom and a male friend of hers as they approached him in line. When taking their tickets, dad made the tiny mistake of assuming mom and her friend were a couple and were "together". This was particularly offensive and embarrassing to my mom, as she observed the proud grin that spread across the face of her flattered companion. "No, we're not together as you may think, sir," she replied tersely. "We are only friends, if that is okay with you?" Little did they realize it then, but mom and dad just had their first tiff!

Fortunately for me, they eventually began to like each other, as they were introduced again a year later through mutual friends. Like a scenario out of a sit-com, dad got his big chance to make things right when he volunteered to act as mom's boyfriend so that she could avoid a professor who was interested in her. By the end of the evening, however, they both found themselves wishing that it wasn't merely an act! Over time, their friendship led to dating, and dating to marriage, which was comprised of two wedding ceremonies: one in India, and the other in Canada.

When I was born in May 1976, they had plans of coming to America, where they'd dreamed of settling down someday to raise their children. Like many other immigrants, it was very difficult for them to decide not to go back home to India, where all of their friends and family awaited their return. My parents were drawn to the greater opportunities the United States had to offer, and didn't want their kids to suffer the hardships they did while growing up. So, like 'two rebels without a clue' in the eyes of their loved ones, mom and dad ended up in snowy Minnesota, all the way on the opposite side of the planet!

Though we never had the support of any relatives being around, we had a truly wonderful, close knit family of four, including my parents, myself and my brother *(and later a fifth member when our dog Gussy came along)* that was kept strong with unconditional love, acceptance, and trust. Whenever I begin to feel I've been cursed in life, I just stop and think how lucky I am to have whom I got for parents. Don't get me wrong now; they are not perfect, and neither was our family, but there was definitely something extra, something very unique and special – that I never understood or appreciated until I became an adult.

Mom and dad are both extremely educated and successful in their respective careers. An electrical engineer and PHD, my father worked with power companies for the past two decades and now consults for them. My mother is a licensed psychologist and also a PHD in her field, working in private practice, mostly with children and families. Although very dedicated to their jobs, my brother and I were always the number one priority to my parents. In fact, mom turned down several great career opportunities to spend her time raising us children.

Almost exactly four years later, my brother was born in April 1980, and her hands were full with two naughty, yet lovable boys. To everyone's delight, he and I got along great from the very beginning, and I do mean that literally. In a story repeated a thousand times by my mom, when I first saw my baby brother at the hospital I held him in my arms and kissed him, causing a few of the nurses to break down and cry. They were touched at how unconditional my love for him was and surprised to see such a genuine display of emotion from a four-year-old child. Their parting words to us were, "You have such a wonderful family."

The words of those nurses have been repeated numerous times over the years by friends as well as countless others who have viewed our family dynamics. What made it so special is how my parents valued and respected our feelings, and the focus that they placed on honest, open communication. Democracy was also a big concept stressed at our house, and we often voted as a family to decide what to go do for fun. In fact, we were so democratic that the three of us outvoted dad in deciding to adopt our dog, Gussy, in 1985! Although against the idea at first, dad grew to love and cherish Gussy as much as the rest of us. Over time they became Monday night football buddies and could be caught on the rocking chair together, both soundly asleep for hours in front of the T.V.

Such good memories fill my heart with happiness and keep my soul warm to this day. Spending quality time together was the most important thing to my parents. Mom and Dad always tried to be with us in person, regardless of the activity, event, or occasion. They were very accepting of our thoughts and ideas and never compared us at all. Without question, we knew they'd be there to protect and support us, regardless of what came our way.

As a result of this shared upbringing, my brother and I were the best of friends and had the most wonderful times. Mom laughs when she recalls how my brother would frequently call me a "little daddy!" For much of the time I lived up to this title with natural ease and pleasure, as the two of us spent the bulk of our childhood time together. I would always come up with creative new games for us to play, embedded with some all-important lesson that I wanted him to learn. The life and personality we put in our toys still amazes us all to this day! To summarize, our home was a wonderland filled with love where our dreams always seemed within reach.

However, this is not to say that things were always bright and rosy. No family is perfectly functional, and ours certainly isn't! As it turned out, there were many tough issues we were forced to face and deal with throughout the years, but when it came right down to the really big stuff, our folks never let us down. There was no divorce or extramarital affairs. There was no abuse or neglect of any kind. Just as important, we never once felt that our parents' affection was something we needed to earn.

So when I think back to my childhood today, I feel blessed to have had such a healthy and joyful upbringing. It is like a great gift I've already enjoyed, but have also just begun to unwrap; a most wonderful gift that would help me survive the hardships I was destined to face.

CHAPTER TWO

EARLY SIGNS OF TROUBLE

"I think God gave people mental illnesses so that we would conquer them over time and become stronger."

10 yr. old friend living with Bipolar Disorder.

In the aftermath of any tragedy or disaster, the universal question we ask ourselves is what could have possibly been done to prevent it from happening? Or more constructively, what can we do now to prevent it from happening again? In the case of OCD, whether for myself or anyone else, it is extremely difficult to come up with any definite answers. Since OCD is caused by a chemical imbalance in the brain, it is often passed down in genes from one generation to another. I also believe that traumatic stress can dictate, to quite an extent, the manner in which this illness plays out for an individual.

The onset of my OCD came right around the age of sixteen, which research shows is a typical age for people with this predisposition to become overwhelmed with symptoms. While there were traumatic experiences in my life *(that I'll discuss in the next chapter)* that I strongly believe helped to fuel the fire, I now realize that from a very young age I was already showing early signs of trouble. Unfortunately for me, my family and I were unable to recognize these warning signals and identify my potential for developing OCD. While catching this illness early on cannot stop it from occurring, knowledge is priceless and can save someone from years of needless suffering, which I could not prevent for myself.

From the beginning I was an extremely emotional and sensitive child, deeply intrigued and affected by the complex world around me. Along with being stubborn and rigid, my desires were strong and my passions ferocious. The earliest example of these traits is one I cannot remember on my own, having occurred when I was just two years old and at Circus World in Orlando, Florida with my parents. Of all the attractions available there to tiny consumers like me, there was one merry-go-round in particular that I had my heart set on riding. It was all I could think about that day, and when we realized it had been shut down for repairs I was devastated. Absolutely devastated! Though

Mom and Dad tried patiently for the next half an hour to distract my attention, their valiant efforts proved to be in vain. While many children in my predicament would have broken down and cried, my reaction seemed to show an understanding that it would serve no purpose to do so. Instead, I just sat on a nearby bench and stared sadly at the ride that had broken my heart. In recalling this vivid memory today, my parents are struck at how difficult it was for me to get over the disappointment and be able to move on to enjoying something else.

While this infamous "merry-go-round incident" could be written off as an attention-seeking tactic of a typical 2yr.old child, it was rather a genuine glimpse of how hard it could be for me to deal with disappointments in life. Gradually we began to see a pattern emerging; that for me, letting go of things, or adapting to changes in general, posed a significant challenge. Though this was not a clear indication of my potential to have OCD, the experience came to serve as a calling card for the problems that lay ahead.

Perhaps the best example came a couple of years later when I started going to school. Again, it was a case of letting go of what was familiar and making a change in my life. I can't recall having much trouble in nursery school or kindergarten, although my mother remembers my kindergarten teacher telling her that I was a "worry wart." What I remember is the fear and heartache I felt when I finally began the first grade. It was different from the kindergarten experience, in that I was now away from home the entire school day instead of just the afternoons. I'm still not sure what precisely scared me so much, but I remember feeling as though I was being forced to leave what I knew was safe and join a world of total strangers. It was like being sent off to summer camp, or even being hauled off to prison! As extreme as that sounds, it's exactly how I felt each day when I waved goodbye to my mom. This was serious enough that my teachers even reported it back to my parents, telling them how I would cry off and on and feel unable to cope.

Fear of doing something, or learning something new remains a big issue for me. Being a die hard perfectionist sure doesn't help matters any! Perfectionism itself, I believe, is a very common trait found in most people with OCD. Regardless of the nature of an individual's symptoms, having an "all or nothing" mentality usually comes with the territory. It certainly did in my case, along with viewing things in our world in terms of being either black or white *(extremely good or extremely bad)*, without taking into consideration all the countless shades of gray in between. Such a thinking pattern can set a person up for repeated failures and frustrations, as they are often unable to meet their own excessive expectations. This, as it did in my case, can lead to overwhelming feelings of guilt, which I believe are also extremely common in people with OCD.

Eventually I made the adjustment to being away from home, although it took me considerably longer than most others to get to that point. However, once I did, signs of obsessive-compulsive behaviors slowly began to emerge. Perhaps the earliest example was my little green eraser. Oh how I loved my little green eraser! It was by far my favorite of all the supplies that I kept in my desk at school. During class I found immense satisfaction in chipping away at the eraser with my fingernails, causing tiny pieces to fall on my clothes, chair, and the carpet beneath my desk. I could never figure out why it felt so good to chip my eraser apart. Looking back, it probably began for me as a typical nervous habit, a means by which to distract myself from the discomfort of being at school.

But like all great romances, over time this love also blossomed into something more! Soon the erasers at the ends of my #2 pencils were also fair game for my madness. The game, however, came to a screeching halt one morning when I looked into my desk and couldn't find my little green eraser. Turns out Mrs. Peterson, my first grade teacher, had taken the eraser away! Upon confronting her about this, she told me she would only give it back when and if I could promise not to chip it apart. In retrospect, this could have been an excellent opportunity for adult intervention. Had my teacher been somewhat educated about OCD, she could have reported the behavior to my parents or discussed it with someone at the school. Instead, it was simply viewed as a strange and quirky habit; a troublesome one that left tiny eraser bits lying all over the carpet.

Over time, this same need began to emerge in other areas. I remember being out with my dad one afternoon when I accidentally chipped some skin off the side of one of my thumbs. Suddenly, I was feeling that same old urge again, and began to chip away relentlessly at the skin on the top of my thumbs and fingers. I guess this was a step up the old OCD ladder, since no Mrs. Peterson could come and take my fingers away from me! Over time my parents came to notice this peculiar habit and would lecture me not to do it. Although involved and aware, they were simply naïve in this area, as most people are, and didn't know what the strange behavior might be trying to imply. While my mom had a degree in psychology and returned to work when we were older, even she didn't really know all that much about OCD.

Besides, a lot of the odd habits that can be signs of OCD are inherently common among the general population. An excellent example would be the need to do certain things in a particular manner. Though this can pertain to just about any area of life, common examples include: how a person arranges their clothes, sets the dinner table, or goes about cleaning the house. Repeated checking would be another good example. I'm sure we've all observed similar characteristics in ourselves as well as others. For most folks it is merely a passing fixation; while for a smaller percentage of us it can become a life-consuming obsession. For as long as I can remember, I have felt utterly compelled to do things in a particular manner for no apparent logical reason. Simply put, it would feel unbearably "wrong and uncomfortable" to do it any other way! In sharing this, it is certainly not my intention to frighten parents should they observe such behaviors in their children. Remember, almost everyone experiences quirky habits or obsessive tendencies at some point in life, and the vast majority by far do not develop OCD! Rather, it is a matter of being informed and keeping watch for obsessive patterns, which may grow and increase over time.

Slowly but surely, my obsessive behavior patterns were continuing to grow. It seemed as though one odd habit would replace, or even join the others, almost like someone was lying in wait with the next one ready to go. Somewhere around this time as a youth, I developed a strange need to frequently spit when I was playing outside. This time, a neighbor, the mom of one of my friends, noticed and brought it to my mother's attention. My mom, in turn, lectured me on the complexities of spitting, explaining that it was rude and that I shouldn't be doing it in public. When questioned as to why I did it, she remembers I didn't seem to have an answer. Regretfully today, she concluded back then that I was trying to misbehave or get attention. Although I don't clearly remember how I responded to her questions, I do remember feeling embarrassed and wanting to ignore the whole issue.

Embarrassment very well illustrates the mixed blessing of having personal insight experienced by those suffering from OCD. As a child (and later an adult), it's hard when you know you're doing things others see as being odd and weird, especially when you also see it as such but still feel compelled to do it! As a result, you seldom want to acknowledge such embarrassing problems and keep the strange needs to yourself. Sadly, it is through this barrier of naivety and shame that the illness can continue to thrive undetected.

In stark contrast to the habits of chipping my skin and spitting, I was also extremely obsessive about cleanliness. From a young age, I would always flush the toilet with my elbows and use them on the faucet when washing my hands. I can actually remember a time when my dad saw me and decided to challenge the act! He told me to use my hands when flushing the toilet, and on the faucet while using the sink. I remember how the concept horrified me, but he insisted that I do it that time. However, when he wasn't around and watching, I quickly went back to my usual ways. As a child, I would also wash my hands repeatedly until I had very dry skin, all because of a lingering feeling that they were somehow still unclean.

But nothing else could begin to compare with my strong fear of germs and disease. While most kids might have been reading more age-appropriate materials, I would have my nose in an encyclopedia, learning which diseases could kill me. A friend of the family caught me reading a health guide for parents, when I was merely an eight-year-old child! As I grew older, fears in this area led to my experiencing full-blown panic attacks.

Tragically, health related concerns were nurtured by my overprotective mother, who also appeared to display some common signs of OCD. She was extremely particular about avoiding germs and disease, always telling us to wash our hands and take great measures to avoid getting sick. In the years after identifying and learning about my illness, we've gone through ugly stages where I blamed mom directly for causing my mental disorder! My brother and I both remember how obsessive she was, and can be, especially when it comes to keeping us healthy and shielding us from harm at all costs.

Fortunately, I have evolved beyond blaming my mother for something that she alone could have never created. However, in retrospect, there are many things I wish we could have known and done before this illness consumed me. Since I cannot change the past, it is my hope to save another individual from enduring a similar future. OCD may not be preventable, but our ignorance certainly is, and ignorance can play a significant role in the development of this disease.

So, too, can traumatic life experiences, as I would very soon come to learn.

CHAPTER THREE
THE BULLYING BREAKDOWN

"The simple act of treating others as we would like to be treated remains a major work in progress, with a long, long way to go."

I can see it any time I look out my back window, but it usually doesn't bother me much. Besides, it looks so small now, and so different and so changed after all these years. On a typical weekday afternoon, I can hear the euphoric sounds of laughter and excitement coming from the direction of its playground, and when I am returning to my house a certain way, I can see the big red banner across the front of it with the words "Respect and Responsibility" printed in capital letters - a positive expression of values and morality that fills me with mixed emotions. For it is the elementary school I attended as a child, from Kindergarten through the sixth grade, in a time when 'respect and responsibility' weren't emphasized nearly enough.

If I could summarize the most negative aspect of my life while growing up with just one word, it would definitely be 'school.' It's as sad as it is true, but school really was like a prison for me; perhaps at first for irrational reasons, but soon for some terribly rational ones. Harassment in schools, having finally come to light through an epidemic of fatal violence, was a very little known or cared about issue back when I was a kid. Regardless, the impact that it had in my case, even all these many years later, continues to live on within me everyday of my life. This is so because tragically, being bullied helped to trigger the onset of my illness and determined to quite a shocking extent the manner in which it played out.

Looking back on it all today, I am grateful that my parents chose to settle down in the United States. Growing up in India probably would have been harder for many reasons, and I generally feel at peace with the decision that they made. Leaving one's homeland has consequences that may not be seen right away, such as having to grow up 'appearing' to somehow be different from everyone else.

This appearance was very ironic considering what my family believed. Unlike many who immigrate to the U.S., my parents were completely Americanized and lived fully the American way. However, I was often viewed in the eyes of my peers with ignorance and contempt. At a stage where children alienate others based on the slightest difference, I realize now in retrospect I had a lot to offer. It also didn't help that I was an innocent, rather anxious, very well behaved boy with no concept of how to deal with malicious cruelty or aggression. On the contrary, my sensitivity to the harassment and my failure to just let it go likely made me an even better target.

Although some older kids picked on me, my problems were primarily with children my own age. Typically, they stemmed from my ethnic background, unusual name, and physical appearance. At my elementary school in conservative Minnesota in the early 1980s, I was one of the only dark-haired kids with a darker skin complexion. Furthermore, I was one of the very, very precious few whose parents were immigrants from India and had grown up on the opposite end of the planet. Not being either black or white, I captured the unwanted fascination of many who wanted to know *what* I was!

Along with the well-intentioned questions regarding where my parents were originally from, there were many cruel comments and rude observations commonly directed my way. For example, I vividly remember kids making fun of the color of my skin, often referring to me as being an "ugly, dirty, brown man from Ethiopia." Now, there's nothing insulting about being Ethiopian, but it was the way they would say it, with such callous disregard, even after I asserted that my parents were originally from India! It just didn't seem to matter. Besides, it showed exactly what they thought about Ethiopians, how they had somehow come to view this group as being unworthy of basic respect. I also recall being teased repeatedly while watching a film in class about Native Americans. Throughout the video, these same kids kept hitting their mouths with their hands, attempting to make what they considered to be 'Native American noises', all the while turning to me and saying stuff like, "Hey, that's you! That stupid, ugly Indian there looks just like you!"

Another example of harassment based on my appearance would be the relentless ripping that I took about my hair. In addition to having dark skin, I was cursed with having more facial and body hair than most other people my age. "Why does your hair grow so much?" or "Oh my God, man, you need to shave! WHY THE HELL DON'T YOU SHAVE?!" were common reactions from countless people over a number of years. I also remember frequently being called a "hairy monkey," a "hairy ape," and a "hairy ball of shit."

Though taunted much more by males, perhaps the most humiliating incident I can remember involved a cheerleader known for her snotty disposition. While teasing me about my body hair, she bluntly stated in front of others, "I bet your dick is really hairy too," and was kind enough to pause and conclude her thoughts by saying, "not that I would ever want to see it!"

Right along with my physical appearance, my full name proved to be a major source of entertainment to many. Had I grown up back in India, the name 'Sumit Sagar Mukherjee' probably wouldn't have stood out at all, but growing up here, it was unheard of, not to mention impossible for people to pronounce (oh go ahead, I'm not listening... give it a try right now!). In fact, I can still remember how embarrassed I felt when a teacher would take attendance. As they would read off the students' names and work their way to the Ms, I would start to feel that familiar tension building up in my chest. It probably didn't help that I wasn't the only one anticipating what was about to happen. "Oh, here comes your name... they're about to mess up your name again!" were remarks commonly directed my way by fellow classmates - sometimes with friendly, good-natured humor, but often with taunting and disrespect.

Looking back on it now, some of these classroom memories are funny even to me. For example, like how we all knew when the teacher had reached my name, due to the sudden pause in their reading and the confusion upon their face. Then after a few seconds of silence (and long, deep breaths on the part of the teacher), he or she would continue with something like, "Ohhhhhh boy... oh my God... ummm let's see here... is it... Sammmeeeett, uhhhh, ummmm... Muuuuk, Muuuuk... oh how do you say your last name?" By this point, everyone would be laughing, and I would regrettably begin my usual, well-practiced routine of explanation.

"Ah, I actually just go by Sumi... S-u-m-i, and my last name is pronounced just like it sounds, Muk-her-jee," I would typically say, as every pair of eyes remained fixed upon me. If I was lucky enough, it would end right there, but depending on the teacher's curiosity I might have to go into further detail. Some would want to know more about where my family originally came from. While my teachers probably only had the best of intentions, I would have been much more comfortable without the focus on me!

Unfortunately, it didn't stop there, because, for lack of a better term, far too many people became obsessed with saying my name. If I had a dollar for every time someone would come up to me and say, "HEY, DON'T SUE-ME, SU-MI," (each thinking they were the first to invent the clever phrase) I probably would have earned enough money to retire! Well beyond that brilliant one liner, people just seemed to love saying my name to me, over, and over, and over again. "SUMI, SUMI, SUMI, SUMI, SUMI!" scores of people would shout and sing at me while passing by in the halls. My middle and last name were also fair game for the ripping, as people called me "cigar," mispronounced my last name, and added the 't' at the end of my first name after I asked them to stop.

My clothing attire while going to school often didn't help matters at all. Being somewhat overprotective, mom always made sure that I wore a hat, gloves, scarf, boots, and snowsuit when it was cold. While mom only had the best of intentions, the outcome could not have been worse. Sadly, dressing this way got me thoroughly teased and made me stand out even more.

With all this stuff going on, it shouldn't come as a shock that I struggled in school and had a hard time staying focused. Towards the end of elementary school, my parents had me evaluated by a psychologist to see if I had disabilities or issues to be addressed. Even after several meetings, she couldn't come up with a definite answer. One thought she had, however, was that I might be too young for my grade. Unlike some other students, I had started Kindergarten when I was just five years old. Following evaluations, she strongly suggested that my parents make me repeat the sixth grade the next year.

At the time this occurred, elementary school consisted of Kindergarten through grade six, while the next level called junior high had grades 7-9, and senior high, as it was then called, had grades 10-12. When I completed the sixth grade at age 12 in 1988, it was the year that junior high was changing into middle school, and would now have grades 6-8. Senior high, meanwhile, transformed into high school, hosting grades 9-12. So, having completed the sixth grade at an elementary level, my parents decided that I should repeat it again at the new middle school.

A LIFE INTERUPTED

Having me repeat the sixth grade, alongside the same group of students, proved to be a recipe for major disaster. During my first few months at the middle school, I was taunted by almost everyone I came into contact with. On the bus, in the hallways, and in classes it was always the same damn thing: "Sumi flunked the sixth grade! Sumi flunked the sixth grade! SUMI FLUNKED, SUMI FLUNKED, SUMI FLUNKED!" People from the grade I had been in, as well as the class in which I was held back, tormented me relentlessly almost everyday of my life. It didn't matter how many times I explained what had actually happened. In their minds I had clearly flunked the sixth grade and deserved to be treated like dirt.

Always there and involved in my life, my parents counseled me through my troubles during these difficult years. They were there at my side on many occasions asking the school for assistance (we even explored attending a private school once, but it didn't seem any better). Our efforts, along with standing up to the bullies, did not always work as we hoped.

While the flunking thing gradually faded with time, the bullying continued for years. Even much later in high school, my ethnicity made me a target. During my freshman year, a group of sophomores and a senior, most of whom I'd never met, came after me with a vengeance. Along with putting condoms and sexual notes into my locker, they covered it with shaving cream and wrote my first name across it! After I reported this to the principal, they began to follow me to all of my classes and yell out my name in the halls. At one point, the leader of the group made a negative reference to where I originally came from. It took several more trips to the principal's office to get them to stop altogether.

Only after my freshman year did the harassment start to subside. From then on it became more subtle, but nonetheless lingered the next three years. In this terribly shallow environment comprised of popular clicks, I was treated by most like an outcast who never fit into the high school world.

When I think about it today, it's difficult to summarize all the different ways in which being bullied has affected my life. Yes, the impact has become more distant with time, since adults don't typically 'bully' one another in the ways that kids often do. Even though I'm no longer being harassed by other people, post traumatic stress disorder

(PTSD) remains a major part of my life. To this day I still have nightmares about all of the shit that I went through in school.

Over many years time, my self-esteem was shaken to its very core by the conduct of my peers. This resulted in the development of tremendous self-doubt and insecurity within me, both of which are prerequisites for Obsessive-Compulsive Disorder.

For example, I feel awkward around people at times for no apparent logical reason, as though every move I make is being harshly judged by others around me. I often find myself striving unduly hard to impress everyone in the room. This usually only makes me feel more insecure, and at times I will fumble my words. I also often feel unattractive, not dressed right, never good enough, and weird. I have to work very hard to convince myself that none of these things are true.

Above everything else, the most difficult aspect of the bullying breakdown is one I have yet to fully disclose: it is the previously mentioned connection that all this would have to my OCD.

CHAPTER FOUR
DESCENDING INTO DARKNESS OF DOUBT

"OCD is widely known by many as being the 'Doubting Disease.' From nearly two decades of personal experience, I can readily say this is true."

I remember it like it was yesterday, even though it took place more than fifteen years ago. I had just turned sixteen and was a freshman in high school. It was my birthday month of May, and the year was 1992. Perhaps I can't forget it because of the fear and doubt that consumed my soul. Or maybe it's because ever since that troubling moment, what I hoped was a freak occurrence has become a way of life for me.

Yes, it's been many years, but I'll never forget sitting in Mrs. DeLapp's ninth grade social studies class that morning at the high school. About four desks behind me sat Brad Wilson, a hyper-active kid who liked to rough house and slap people on the back of the head. Of course he did it more to me, because unlike most others it would bother me more, and I'd always try to chase him and hit him back. Looking back on it now, Brad wasn't nearly as cold or cruel as many of the people who picked on me. Regardless, he offended my sensitivities and threatened my sense of manhood, and regretfully I simply wasn't able to let it go.

The previous day in gym class, Brad and I had a confrontation, I believe caused by my trying to get revenge on him for an earlier incident. In short, I smacked him on the back of the head and took off running, with him right behind me in close pursuit. Although he chased me all over the gymnasium for several minutes, a teacher intervened and Brad was unable to hit me back.

For the rest of that afternoon I remember feeling completely elated, like being high on cloud nine from having finally gotten revenge. Later that evening, my satisfaction was interrupted by a very strange feeling; a troubling thought that perhaps Brad *had* in fact succeeded in hitting me back! This sudden doubt struck me as odd and disturbing, to say the very least, since I *KNEW* darn well that he had *NOT* been successful. Interestingly, the reality of the situation didn't ease the uncomfortable feeling. In fact, the more I tried to convince myself of what I knew to be true, the stronger those feelings of doubt began to grow.

The next thing I vividly remember thinking was, "What if Brad had succeeded in hitting me back, but I was simply in denial about it???" Weird as it was, all I could think about now was how revenge on Brad seemed far too good to be true. Could I actually be in denial? Could I be losing my grip on reality? Could I have lied to myself about what happened just to make myself feel better? Regardless of the answers to those nagging questions, I wasn't feeling better anymore!

Not too surprising then that the next morning in social studies class my mind wasn't on academics. Instead, I kept turning to look behind me, to see if Brad was about to slap me on the back of the head. Throughout that hour I kept having these staggering doubts, wondering every few minutes whether Brad had just hit me. I even concentrated on whether or not I felt pain at the back of my head, as a way of disproving the irrational belief. As that hour slowly passed by, the doubts only grew stronger. Finally, when the bell rang ending the period, I was the first one to burst out the door and bolt up a flight of stairs.

Yet when I reached the top I was completely overwhelmed by the feeling that Brad had just hit me! This time the doubt was the biggest it had ever been, and I spent several minutes standing in the hallway trying to prove to myself that it hadn't happened. As others passed me by on their way to class, I concentrated intensely on whether or not I felt any pain in my head, and used whatever circumstantial evidence I could think of to disprove the belief. "Okay, if Brad had hit me, he probably would have said something too, and I don't remember him saying anything, therefore he couldn't have possibly hit me," is just one example of my futile attempt to prove what I already knew. As I continued to wrestle with these doubts throughout the day, I remember wondering if there would ever come a time when I would truly understand what had happened to me. Though a day of revelation would eventually come, it was still many long years away, and while I hoped this strange intrusion was a one shot deal, it had merely been a preview of what lay ahead.

Mercifully, I was able to enjoy most of the summer before the darkness of doubt would embrace me again. In August 1992, right before the start of tenth grade, I got confirmation that what happened in May was not a one-time thing. When packing my suitcase for a family vacation, I felt the irrational need to keep unzipping it just to be "sure" that my items were still inside. Each time that I confirmed this and zipped up my bags, I was overwhelmed by uncertainty and needed to check them again. "What if you imagined your items are inside, when actually they are not?" was the doubtful thought that kept popping back into my mind every time.

Throughout our trip that summer, doubts about my most basic perceptions continued to mount. Suddenly, I could no longer take for granted what I heard, saw, or touched in my environment as being real. I could merely glance at an item in our hotel room and doubt whether it was actually there, or if I had imagined its presence. I also started doubting whether I'd done things I viewed as being dangerous or going against my morals and values.

For example, I recall one evening when my parents were drinking beer out on the balcony. Just as they stepped inside, I began to doubt whether I had taken a sip of their drinks! Fearful of intoxication, the idea that I'd actually taken a drink was extremely disturbing to me. While I knew deep inside that I hadn't really done it, the doubt was as strong as could be. Only after exhaustive mental reviewing could I safely conclude that it hadn't occurred.

Upon returning home from our trip, I found myself overwhelmed by a frightening sense of depression. Unsure of the cause, I figured it was from being back in Minnesota and nearing the start of tenth grade. I slowly began to realize that it cut even deeper than that. Something about me was changing, and I just wasn't sure what it was. All of a sudden, I felt an inner emptiness spreading throughout my being. I tried to stay physically close to my loved ones, not wanting to be alone in any room of the house. I was also more panicky for no apparent reason, and began to worry about things that should not have provoked concern. "What if I start crying and just cannot stop?" was one of many random, anxious thoughts that crept through my mind.

As I started the tenth grade in Sept. 1992, I was a different person from the relatively carefree kid who had gotten A(s) and B(s) the previous year. My mind was now clouded with irrational doubts, and much of my time went into convincing myself that these were not valid concerns. Ironically, just as the years of harassment were coming to an end, I found myself burdened by this new set of troubles. Before long, I came face to face with the same kind of doubts I encountered over the summer.

Though stronger and more prevalent than before, they all involved irrational doubts about my perceptions of what was around me. As I passed another student in the hallway, I would suddenly wonder whether or not they had elbowed me in the stomach, or if they had punched me on the shoulder, or even if I had slapped them on the head! While I knew these things hadn't happened, the thoughts came so quick and were so specific that I struggled to convince myself they weren't for real. The closer I was physically to the persons when I passed them, the stronger the doubt would be that they *might* have just hit me. Naturally, my doubts were often the strongest if the person that I walked by was someone with whom I'd had trouble with in the past.

This did not always have to be the case. Soon enough, I began experiencing the same doubts when passing by teachers, most of whom I'd never had in class. As I'd pass a male teacher in the hallway, I'd suddenly wonder whether he had fondled my genital area with his hand! Such sexual thoughts and images were extremely repulsive to me, and I couldn't move on with my day until I was 'sure' that they hadn't occurred. "Did I just kiss that guy there on the lips? Did my hand touch that person's penis? Did I just suck that guy's dick?" are just some examples of the kinds of disgusting doubts I was frequently having.

Though unknown to me at the time, the harder I tried to resist such thoughts, the stronger and faster they came. Though not exclusively sexual in nature, they involved doubts about seeing unsettling things that I *knew* weren't really there. For example, as I'd walk down a hallway and turn a corner, I could suddenly doubt whether I had seen a naked child covered with blood! Each thought was very detailed and specific in nature, although the images/scenarios appeared completely random. It was like the devil hijacked my imagination to play a most tormenting game. Poisoned with irrational doubt, I'd feel compelled to walk back around the corner and check that same spot again. In fact, checking seemed to be the only way to help myself feel less anxious. Yet the more I repeated these actions, the quicker such doubts would return. It wasn't long before these thoughts were occurring dozens of times each day, causing me to hang around for hours after school rechecking different parts of the building.

As my illness continued to progress, my doubts only grew more frightening and bizarre. Perhaps the worst occurred one evening as I was sitting alone in my bedroom. It was in relation to something that had happened earlier that day at school in speech class, where another male student, who was rumored to be gay, had given a talk in support of gay rights. Being interested in the issue, I stayed after class to have a discussion with him. We had a brief conversation, just the two of us alone in the room, in which he asserted again that he wasn't gay, but was merely in support of gay rights.

That night in bed, I suddenly had a thought that maybe I had given this guy my phone number and address, that maybe he *was* in fact gay, and that maybe he was about to come over to my house and have anal sex with me!!! ABSOLUTELY TERRIFIED at the prospect of this – especially with my fear of getting AIDS – I tried desperately all night to convince myself that none of these things were true. The doubt was so amazingly strong this time that I felt the need to take preventive measures. The next morning while showering, I specially rinsed out my anal area with water for several minutes, to be 'certain' that there wasn't any sperm inside and that I wasn't about to get AIDS.

As I sit here and write about this now, it's hard to believe that such irrational doubts once had so much control over me. When I think back to those most dreadful years, I shudder to remember how awful it was. There would soon be many more instances in which I did similar things, and to realize I had only hit the tip of the iceberg still makes me wonder how I ever survived.

CHAPTER FIVE
BIZARRE THOUGHTS, BEHAVIORS AND RITUALS

"The true definition of insanity is to repeat the same behaviors and expect a different outcome."

Generally speaking, teenage years are a difficult stage in life for everyone, regardless of your gender, who you are, or where you come from. It is a time of great transition, personal change, and revelation. It is also a time when one seriously considers, perhaps for the first time ever, who they really are and who they would like to be. So tell me, what would you do at this critical point in your life if you fear you are going crazy and might need to be sent away???

It is perhaps a morbid question most people don't want to think about; one of those worst case scenarios we simply assume cannot happen to us. I, too, once thought the same way, but sadly, this was the exact dilemma I was forced to face during my teenage years. As bizarre thoughts, behaviors, and rituals continued to increase, I found myself moving towards the conclusion that I was going insane.

In retrospect, I now see the irony in my analysis of myself at that time, as people with OCD are about as far from being crazy as anyone can get! Rather, we are typically intelligent, rational human beings with very high morals and values. As a naïve teenager, my symptoms had me believing otherwise. All I had to do was imagine my reaction if a friend was experiencing this. In my youthfulness and ignorance, I would have thought they were losing their mind! As a result, I was far too afraid to tell my parents what was going on. It seemed, for the first time ever, that I would be facing this bully alone.

Ironically, being a psychologist's son only served to strengthen the terror within me. Curious about my condition, I'd search for some clues and answers in my mother's psychology books. These well-intentioned efforts led me straight in the wrong direction, and I mistakenly came to believe that I was a paranoid schizophrenic! As a result, I felt paralyzing fear and helplessness in the face of this grim diagnosis.

With each passing day it seemed that things would only get worse. Around this time, I began to experience intrusive thoughts about human male genitalia. These in particular were triggered by news about cannibal serial killer Jeffrey Dahmer, whose grisly case was all over the media at the time. Always fascinated with criminals, my illness made me doubt whether I was "crazy" like Jeffrey Dahmer. As a result, I began to imagine seeing severed penises and testicles in my house, outside, and at school! While I knew that these items were not really there, that fact didn't help me at all. My doubts compelled me to recheck any spot where I thought that I might have seen them.

Much like my earlier symptoms, this one, too, only worsened with time. Soon, I began to imagine seeing severed body parts in my plate while eating meals! The harder I tried to push out such revolting thoughts, the more frequently they attacked me. At times it was difficult for me to eat at all, as I found myself sickened by my own imagination. To quell such doubts, I would take pieces of chewed up food out of my mouth and examine them, to be *sure* that they weren't genitalia! Other common thoughts in this area included doubts about seeing sharp objects, black colors, drugs, blood, sperm, insects, or hair in my food. Anything disgusting or harmful in nature had a place in this torturous game.

These basic principles seemed to apply to a wide variety of symptoms. For example, I began to imagine seeing intruders being inside my house. This occurred some during the day, but most frequently at night. Anytime I turned a corner or walked out of a room, I would doubt whether I had seen someone and needed to check there again. At times this would compel me to inspect every inch of the house.

Around this time I also developed new irrational fears, which could sometimes trigger panic attacks. For example, as I'd walk through my house I'd imagine seeing water flowing out of random objects and flames around every corner. I also became very fearful of heights, so much that I'd be scared of going up to my bedroom! For whatever reason, I was petrified that if I went too high up some force might sweep me away. This specific fear would lead to frightening panic attacks, where I worried my house might spin in circles or even roll away.

This apparent fear of motion also occurred when I rode in a car. After exiting the vehicle, I'd worry that the ground below me might start moving under my feet! Other times I found myself overwhelmed by counting rituals, where I felt compelled to count to a certain "safe" number before I could try to move on.

Another area of my life that was destroyed by this illness was exercise. Having worked out regularly (push-ups, sit-ups, squats, jogging, etc.) since I was eleven years old, I had managed to keep myself in excellent physical shape. Amazingly, my sickness found a clever way to ruin this for me as well. Rather than reverting to the bizarre, my thoughts while doing exercise began to center around perfectionism. Okay, make that *extreme* perfectionism! In other words, if my hands weren't a certain 'perfect' distance from one another while doing push-ups, then I felt as though the workout hadn't helped me at all! Soon this principle applied to other exercises as well, and what was once an enjoyable pastime quickly became a tremendous frustration. Eventually, I figured if I couldn't do it right, I might as well not do it at all. After several years of hard work and dedication, I simply quit working out. In this way I felt I had freed myself from the daunting prospect of failure.

With the passage of time, the distress from all of my symptoms took a devastating toll. As tenth grade turned into eleventh, and eleventh into twelfth, my grades took a serious nosedive and I lost all interest in school. Instead, I spent most of my time in a fantasy world trying to cope with the pain of real life. By my senior year of high school, I was failing almost all of my classes. If it weren't for the kindness of my teachers and A TON of help from my dad, I never would've left that living hell with a diploma!

That's because my senior year was, to date, the most awful year of my life. Along with my growing illness, I had several negative experiences with girls that left me feeling depressed. Overwhelmed with despair, my parents had me see a therapist to help me deal with these issues. Sadly, this intervention failed to expose the OCD symptoms I was trying to conceal. Though my family could clearly tell I had a hard time getting around, I was able to pass this slowness off as part of my deep depression. Once again I had succeeded in keeping my frightening condition a secret.

A LIFE INTERUPTED

As my symptoms continued to expand, it felt harder to even consider telling anyone what was going on. During my senior year, I developed a new ritual that made it much tougher to simply move from one spot to another. Every time I took a step with my foot, I would picture the mental image of a bully (someone from my past) at the spot where my foot made contact with the ground! In response to this intrusive thought I'd feel compelled to physically retake that step, and in doing so to mentally neutralize my image of the bully with a positive image.

Interestingly, the positive image I came up with was the face of Geraldo Rivera, who at the time had a popular talk show that I watched every day. Looking back on it now, my mind probably picked Geraldo because of the caring person he portrayed himself to be. Amongst other things, Geraldo appeared strong and extremely self-assured. Facing troubling situations, he offered free counseling to crying victims and spoke out against many forms of oppression.

Unlike most others, this ritual could literally stop me in my tracks and prevent me from moving at all. Sounds pretty crazy now, doesn't it? Well, that's exactly what I thought, too! Like all my other rituals, this one soon spread to cover a variety of different areas. I could be doing something as simple as taking a sip of water, and the moment that my lips made contact with the glass, I would suddenly picture the image of a bully. Soon, any physical activity you can think of, including blinking my eyes, wiggling my toes, or merely breathing, could produce the mental image of a bully and the need to repeat that action. The bullies whose faces I'd imagine were, for the most part, no longer attending my high school. Yet their images felt like a flashback to me and reminded me what I had been through.

When this occurred, I felt like whatever I touched was 'contaminated' with the presence of that individual. At times, the bully's image would be accompanied with an image of a friend or family member, and the strange fear that if I didn't neutralize it, then I may never feel affection for that loved individual again! If you find this stuff difficult to follow as you read it, you can imagine how I felt when it was happening to me.

Other times, I'd look at a loved one and get an image of a bully being inside of them! To neutralize this, I would stare at the individual and perform some physical action (blink my eyes, shake my head, stomp my foot, etc.) while picturing the image of Geraldo entering them. Sometimes a bully's image would come to me in a miniaturized form, while other times it would just be their face in the daunting form of a severed head. There would even be times when the images of two bullies appeared together. These images could also be accompanied by ones of fires burning, water flowing, cars moving, people falling, or anything else that appeared to be outside of my control.

Sadly, these obsessive fears also reached the most personal, intimate areas of my life. At times, while sitting to use the bathroom, my penis would naturally brush against the side of the toilet. Tragically, this physical contact would produce the image of a miniaturized bully being 'inside' of my penis! In response, I feared that my penis wouldn't sexually function correctly if I didn't neutralize the bully's image.

As you can probably imagine, these rituals became exhausting and continued throughout the day. Before long, I could find myself either stepping in the same spot for hours, repeatedly touching a glass to my lips, or bumping my penis on the side of the toilet. It was slavery and imprisonment to the utmost extreme, a degree of control most people probably can't even comprehend. Rituals also occurred while driving and even when I was sound asleep, as I'd dream about doing compulsive behaviors and not being able to stop. The harder I tried, the more difficult it was to neutralize a bully's image. At times, people would catch me engaged in strange behaviors and ask me what the hell I was doing! Embarrassing as it was, this would often be the only thing in the world that could break me away from my pattern.

But by far, I was amazed at how simple and easy it was to hide my compulsive behaviors. Though people could witness my caution and slowness, they had no clue as to what was behind it. One teacher I had in study hall that year was actually impressed with me taking my time! His was the last class of the day, and as soon as the bell rang, everyone was bolting out the door, everyone except for me. I'd always need several more minutes to finish up ritualizing. Once the room had emptied, he would smile with pride and say, "It's so nice to see at least one young man who's not in a hurry to go!"

Friends, in general, provided me the only break in the day from my symptoms, as I couldn't afford to let them see all the crazy looking things I would do. As a result, my hours with them were like magical times during which my disease would back off. Fortunately, my senior year was a period of time when I did have a lot of friends. Most helpful to me was my best friend since the eighth grade named Kyle. Along with having great chemistry, Kyle and I were both unlucky with girls and shared a similar past. While most of our buddies had girlfriends, we were there for one another through the loneliest times. Our special bond lasted for several years after the completion of high school. Although our contact is mainly through Facebook today, I'll always cherish every single moment that we shared. In all likelihood, my amazing friendship with Kyle is what literally helped me hold on and survive. Incredibly, even the most awful years of my life had wonderful memories I'll never forget!

Another great friend who brightened my darkest days was our little dog, Gussy. Over the years I had come to rely on Gussy's unconditional love to deal with the pain in my life. On one occasion while I was ritualizing on my driveway, Gussy got free from my grasp and ran towards the road. A bus just happened to be passing by, but fortunately I was able to scoop him up before he was in any danger. Following the incident, I tried to use this potential risk to Gussy's safety as an incentive to stop me from ritualizing. "This dog is like my child, he depends on me for life and my actions on the driveway could've gotten him killed," I'd say to myself.

Throughout the summer of 1995, I kept using Gussy's life as the sole reason to kick my strange, compulsive habits. Soon I developed a method to quit ritualizing, which in itself became obsessive. Placing a hand on my dog's head, I would repeatedly swear to him, on his life, that I would never, ever, ever ritualize again. Each time that I failed at achieving this goal, my feelings of guilt would dramatically increase. Though my little dog was patient and forgiving through it all, I was far less forgiving with myself! After all, if I couldn't control my actions even to save a dear loved one's life, then what kind of a person did that make me???

Finally, in Sept. 1995, when I started my first job, my symptoms cleared to the point where I actually thought they might never return. Just as sure as the sun will rise, they resurfaced with a vengeance in 1996. It was the same old game all over again, only this time it would be even worse.

CHAPTER SIX
THREATS OF DEATH AND DEMISE

"In the case of Obsessive Compulsive Disorder, the word 'FEAR' represents False Evidence Appearing Real."

Considering my background of anxiety and harassment, the hotel business probably wasn't the best move for me after finishing high school. However, feeling completely burned out, I was willing to work almost any job instead of considering college. So when my father suggested I try hospitality, I felt it was as good a place as any to begin.

The first job I had was in September 1995, at the age of nineteen. I was a lobby attendant at a hotel and really didn't like the work. After being written up a few times, I quit and got a job in October at a bigger hotel, this time working on the front office staff. This job was even harder than the first one, as the training was poor and the environment very stressful. Being scolded by angry guests and uncaring bosses brought back memories of harassment in school. I finally quit that job in March of 1996 and found work at yet another hotel in April.

Ironically, it was during this third job that my OCD symptoms began to re-emerge. In contrast to the previous places, my bosses here were very kind and nurturing. As a result, I seemed to thrive at this job, even making employee of the month in November 1996! Over that summer, my illness inexplicably made a comeback in my life. As much as I tried to deny it, I again found myself having images of bullies and performing countless rituals to neutralize them.

This time there was an additional component to these intrusive thoughts, as though the OCD had consciously decided to up the ante. Along with the image of a bully and a family member, there were threats that if I didn't neutralize it, the bully's image would make something horrible happen to my loved one! Tragic scenarios that accompanied these images included accidents, crashes, illnesses, murder, or anything else awful one can possibly bring to mind. Soon, this threat was followed by an even more frightening one; this time claiming that if I didn't neutralize the bully's image, it would somehow force me to kill my family member!!!

One must understand that through it all, I never heard actual voices making these threats. Rather, it was an inner feeling so specific in nature that it absolutely terrified me. The potential victims of these feared atrocities were always my parents, my brother, and Gussy. In fact, Gussy's image often came up more frequently than the others, as I viewed him as being most vulnerable and unable to call out for help as a human being could do. While I had previously gotten better at resisting ritualizing, threats of death and demise made it all but impossible for me to perceive 'letting go'.

Along with harm to my family, my thoughts soon spread to include awful threats of harm befalling on me. While I rarely ever feared for my own life, the threats I found most concerning had to do with my sexual function. Like most young men, sex was extremely important to me, especially since by this point in my life I had never gotten any! As usual, my illness seemed to know exactly what would bother me the most. Along with the usual image of a miniaturized bully being inside of my penis, there was now a threat that if I didn't neutralize it, that image would somehow force me to cut off my own penis!

Other threats I experienced (if I didn't neutralize) were that any future sex I had might remind me of the bully, that my sexual pleasure might magically go to the bully or that I might be gay and actually want to have sex with the bully! All of these disturbing thoughts would often occur during masturbation, turning my only form of gratification into a marathon of rituals. The humiliation experienced from this intrusion was overwhelming, and showed me how much control the illness had over intimate parts of my life.

The hours I was working at my job didn't help matters any. Ever since finishing high school, I had started a lonely routine of staying up late at night and waking up late in the day. Because my high school experience was so awful, I wanted a schedule completely different from that of my senior year. Therefore, I made sure to work the evening shift at my hotel jobs, from 3-11p.m.

Unfortunately, this schedule provided me a lot of time to ritualize at home while everyone else was asleep. Soon I found myself ritualizing throughout the whole night, often non-stop until 6 o'clock in the morning! If I thought my rituals were exhausting before, I hadn't truly understood the meaning of the word! In addition to everything else, it was hardest to resist doing a ritual right before going to bed, as I feared that my failure to do so could result in me sleepwalking and killing everyone in my sleep! Petrified of waking up to find their bloody corpses, I literally did whatever my illness ordered me to do.

Along with occupying a lot more of my time, my rituals also began to get more painful and intense. For example, if my hand touched the side of the table, and there was an image of a bully, the threats would compel me to touch it again with at least as much force as before. As a result, I'd often end up hurting different parts of my body through repetitive physical actions. In the worst-case scenarios, I would bang my head on a wall, my feet against a desk, or even bump my penis on the side of the toilet to name a mere few! Wherever the image of a bully appeared was fair game for this to occur. Ironically, acknowledging how crazy these behaviors seemed was what kept me somewhat hopeful that I *wasn't* insane. After all, if I can see how irrational my thoughts and actions are, then how can I truly be losing my mind???

In March 1997, after five agonizing years, I finally got the answers I had wanted all along. Before I could think about reaching the top, I'd first have to hit rock bottom. I'd first have to sink to a level so low that I was willing to surrender my secret.

CHAPTER SEVEN

ENDING THE YEARS OF SILENCE

"At the movies, they say silence is golden. In real life, silence can keep the truth hidden and cause immeasurable suffering. If one person reading this finds the courage to break an unhealthy silence, then my years of quiet agony were not all in vain."

Thursday, March 6, 1997 probably seemed like an ordinary day to my colleagues at the Hawthorne Suites Hotel in Edina. For most of them it probably was. On second shift at the front desk it was business as usual, with people checking in and phone calls to answer, but for me, the day marked a dramatic end to a week filled with terror and a secret I'd been hiding for the past five years.

Although my symptoms had tortured me with countless unhappy moments, the first week of March '97 was by far the most awful week of my life. By this point, it seemed like my world was caving in and that my illness would finally destroy me. Barely able to function at all, I now found myself unable to hide my behavior from the people around me.

This proved to be most troublesome at work, especially when I went as far as involving others in performing my rituals! Ricardo, as I will call him, was a lobby attendant unlucky enough to be working that week with me. Before long, he found himself going above and beyond the call of duty, as I instructed him to keep bringing a bag of garbage back to the desk. Though Ricardo was soft spoken and had a very friendly demeanor, I could clearly tell now that he was growing annoyed! While I felt bad about having him do this, I also felt I didn't have another choice. There had been an "image" of a bully on a piece of Kleenex I had thrown in the trash. I feared that if I didn't dig it out, retouch it, and throw it back in again, the image might make me kill a family member! In spite of the inconvenience to both Ricardo and myself, I saw resisting as presenting a terrible risk that I just wasn't willing to take.

Equally as bad was when others caught me engaged in obsessive behavior. Throughout that week I looked stressed and confused to my colleagues at the front desk. At times they would catch me stuck in one spot or returning after punching out to finish a ritual. One girl even said to me the worst thing I could have possibly heard; she said, "The way you've been acting lately makes us think you're going nuts!" After five years of keeping silent to avoid that diagnosis, her words sent chills up and down my spine.

So, by Thursday, March 6, I had just about reached the end of my rope. It was turning out to be the worst day yet, so bad that by the end of my shift I couldn't even leave the hotel by myself! With every step I took towards the door there was an image of a bully along with a threat. Having reached my lowest point in five years, I phoned my father to come over to physically walk me out the front doors!

On Friday, March 7, the following day, I was unable to go into work. Instead, I spent the day at home with my parents making plans to meet with Dr. Geistrom, the psychiatrist who had put me on Zoloft for depression during my senior year. With an appointment scheduled for Tuesday morning, I realized now that it was finally time to start talking.

Ironically, with my symptoms being as bad as they were, my long running fear of being hospitalized (if it turned out that I was insane) no longer presented the threat that it had in the past. The fact of the matter was that whether crazy or not, I could barely function at all and was in desperate need of assistance! Being locked up at this point, it seemed, couldn't make my life any worse.

So, that afternoon, while standing in the kitchen, I decided to talk to my dad. He didn't have long to chat however, as he was planning to take my mother out to celebrate her birthday. In the few short minutes that we had together I told him that I had a major problem. Almost immediately, his fatherly instincts kicked in and he slowly turned to look me in the face. "You've been hiding something big from us for a long time now, haven't you?" he surprised me by saying.

Taking a deep breath, I answered, "Yes, Dad, I have been hiding something real big. I've been having many terrible thoughts for some time, but I'm too afraid to tell you what they are."

Looking puzzled and concerned, he went on to ask me, "But you know you can tell us anything, Sumi, so what thoughts could be so awful that you're too afraid to tell us???"

I just looked him in the eyes and didn't say a word. For several seconds neither of us did. Then amazingly, in a moment of truth typically only seen in a Hollywood production, he suddenly blurted out, "Well, Sumi, the worst thought I imagine you could possibly have is that you're going to kill me!" Yeah that's right. That's exactly how it happened. I guess sometimes life really imitates art.

Later that evening, as we sat together in the basement, I slowly, cautiously began to tell my dad about my ordeal. This process was made even harder by the threats that my illness was making. "If you tell him one more word, you're gonna have to kill him!" was the bad, obsessive thought that kept running through my mind. Nevertheless, I somehow kept talking. Somehow; and as the truth gradually trickled out, I was surprised by my dad's reaction. Incredibly, he didn't think that I was crazy at all! In fact, he and mom weren't afraid to sleep in the same house as me, even knowing now how frequently I feared that I might harm them. Instead, their faith in who I was as a person never wavered an inch. To this day, Mom sees my confession as being the best birthday gift of her life.

Although I felt a miraculous sense of relief, I knew I had a long, hard road ahead of me. As it turned out, I wouldn't be the only one affected by this new revelation. Unable to function normally, I had to quit my front desk job at the Hawthorn Suites Hotel. Tragically, it just so happened that right after my sudden departure, the INS (Immigration and Naturalization Service) came to our hotel and removed every worker from the housekeeping department! I later learned that the general manager and sales staff had to scramble cleaning rooms for the guests. Had my departure not been due to a terrible illness, I'm sure they could've used my assistance! Nonetheless, it had finally come time for me to deal with my issues. I realized that I had my own mess to clean up.

On Tuesday, March 11, my dad and I made the trip out to meet with Dr. Geistrom, the psychiatrist from my past. It had been a few years since I'd seen her and you'd better believe I was shitting my pants! After all, she would be the first mental health professional to hear about my illness. What if she thought I was crazy, or what if she just didn't understand?

These basic worries were not alone in troubling me that morning. Along with everything else, the symptoms from my illness were the worst they had ever been. Once again, every move I made was accompanied by the image of a bully along with a threat. It seemed like my illness was physically trying to prevent me from going to the doctor. Even during the drive I found myself battling images of bullies. Eventually, all this mounting pressure was more than I could take, and my dad had to stop on the side of the road so that I could get out and throw up.

Along with all this drama, we ended up getting lost and going the wrong way on an exit, right into oncoming traffic! When we finally made it into the long-sought building, my dad and I raced up the stairs. As we turned every corner on that stairwell, I felt this was the most important day of my life. I felt like we were climbing the steps of a castle, where high at the top stood the cure to my illness.

For whatever reason, I don't remember a lot about our actual meeting. What I do remember, however, was being told by Dr. Geistrom that the strange disease which had consumed my existence was called Obsessive Compulsive Disorder, known in short as OCD.

Oh, and I also remember one other detail. Before leaving her office, I looked deeply into the doctor's eyes and asked her one final question. Having confirmed that I wasn't crazy, I proceeded to inquire, "Is there effective treatment for my OCD?"

With a kind, reassuring smile, she answered me in one word, "Absolutely!." I guess this was the most important day of my life.

CHAPTER EIGHT
UNDERSTANDING THE ENEMY WITHIN

"Understanding an enemy outside of yourself can be a difficult and complex process. But understanding an enemy within you can be an even more remarkable task."

There are some advantages to having a psychologist for a mother. Thus far I had only experienced the downside, such as books about mental illnesses being kept within my reach. When it came time to find a therapist to treat my OCD, I realized I already had one foot inside the door. Using a pamphlet that my mom had listing providers in Minnesota, we searched to find the right person for the tough job that lay ahead.

Eventually, we decided on a psychologist, located only a few miles from my house. The pamphlet listed this psychologist as being an OCD expert and one of the most experienced in dealing with anxiety disorders. After a positive introductory meeting, I began weekly sessions with this psychologist in April 1997. I also placed myself under the care of his colleague and a psychiatrist, who worked in the same building alongside my therapist. In addition to beginning talk therapy, my psychiatrist placed me on the medications Zoloft and Risperdol. Though used as an antipsychotic, small doses of the latter drug have proven helpful with OCD. At last, it seemed as though I was getting the treatment I'd needed for several years.

The first step of this treatment was to learn everything that I could about OCD. Along with starting therapy, I began to read materials pertaining to my illness. What I discovered was how appropriate the diagnosis was for me! As stated on a website called familydoctor.org, OCD is a mental illness that causes people to have unwanted thoughts (obsessions) and to repeat certain behaviors (compulsions) over and over again. Though most people with OCD know their symptoms do not make sense, they strongly feel as though they cannot stop or ignore them.

Sounds a lot like me, now doesn't it? As I continued reading, I learned that obsessions are ideas, images, and impulses that run through a person's mind over and over again. A person with OCD doesn't want to have these thoughts, finding them intrusive and disturbing. Compulsions, also known as rituals, are the behaviors people perform to rid themselves of these awful feelings. More specifically, they are used to neutralize or cancel out the perceived impact left by the bad thoughts. Some common obsessions, as stated on this website, include the following:

- fear of dirt or germs
- disgust with bodily waste or fluids
- concern with order, symmetry (balance), and exactness
- worry that a task has been done poorly, even when the person knows this is not true
- fear of thinking evil or sinful thoughts
- thinking about certain sounds, images, words, or numbers all the time
- need for constant reassurance
- fear of harming a family member or friend

Common compulsions for OCDers listed on the website include the following:

- cleaning and grooming, such as washing hands, showering, or brushing teeth over and over again
- checking drawers, door locks, and appliances to be sure they are shut, locked or turned off
- repeating, such as going in and out of a door, sitting down and getting up from a chair, or touching certain objects several times
- ordering and arranging items in certain ways
- counting over and over to a certain number
- saving newspapers, mail, or containers when they are no longer needed, also known as hoarding
- seeking constant reassurance and approval

As I read through these obsessions and compulsions, I realized I'd experienced all of them at some point, with the exception of hoarding. Obviously, my specialty was having fears of harming my loved ones along with images of bullies and repeating certain actions to 'prevent' this from occurring. Overall as an OCDer, I was really a textbook case. I also discovered that this illness is not a sole result of psychological trauma, but is actually caused by a chemical imbalance in the brain. Psychological trauma however, such as years of relentless bullying from peers, can trigger the illness onset and determine the ways in which it plays out. After years spent fully believing that I was a schizophrenic, I finally understood exactly what had gone wrong with me!

Things continued to progress wonderfully over time with my therapist. He proved to be an excellent therapist and I truly felt lucky to have him. At some point I even playfully nicknamed him the God of OCD! Talking for the first time about my illness really seemed to liberate me. A couple of months after starting therapy, my therapist introduced me to his OCD support group, comprised of other patients he'd been treating throughout the years. I was moved by how understanding they all were of my situation, and how quickly they accepted me into their group. Armed with this new confidence, I began talking more freely about my disease to a number of different people. Amazingly, each person was sympathetic and none of them thought that I was crazy! In fact, almost everyone could relate in some ways to obsessive-compulsive behavior. Around this time, I also started taking classes at a local community college. This was my first attempt since the completion of high school to further my education. At last, it seemed I had managed to put myself back on the right track.

However, doing what was needed to combat my illness still presented a difficult task. As the jubilation from getting help slowly began to fade, I struggled hard to follow through on what I was being taught. Along with taking medication, the treatment used to conquer OCD is called Cognitive Behavioral Therapy. Simply put, it is the process of accepting one's frightful obsessions and declining to perform their compulsive behaviors. In essence, it is a paradox and a tricky one at that. In order to reduce my unwanted bad thoughts, I'd have to stop trying to get rid of them. In sharp contrast to my usual neutralizing, I would need to provoke and encourage such thoughts to frequently enter my mind!

As stated in Lee Baer's revealing book, <u>The Imp Of The Mind – Exploring The Silent Epidemic Of Obsessive Bad Thoughts</u>,

"Anytime we try to force ourselves *not* to think a particular thought, the thought is paradoxically given more energy. By doing so, we are beginning an endless cycle of failed thought suppression and a rebounding of more intense bad thoughts. By stopping thought suppression and letting bad thoughts pass through the mind, those thoughts become less bothersome and less noticed over time."

Along with accepting bad thoughts, the other half of the equation involves not performing compulsive behaviors. One of the major steps used to help a person achieve this goal is a coping tactic known as postponing. Basically, when you have a bad thought and feel the need to ritualize, you postpone doing the compulsion and tell yourself that you'll do it later. You can choose to postpone for just a few minutes or for much longer, like hours or even days at a time. The awesome thing is that whenever you choose to postpone, the strength of your obsessive bad thought slowly begins to fade. In effect, by postponing you increase the likelihood that you will not perform the compulsion! I already knew this to be true from personal experience, as I had used this tactic throughout the years without knowing its significance... that is until then. At last, I was slowly beginning to understand the enemy living within me.

Still, it was not always easy to postpone my compulsions. This was especially true right before going to bed. It was easier during the day to put off compulsions until the night, since I knew I would be awake and felt in control of myself. As a result, this led to more freedom from my symptoms throughout the day. In fact, when postponing I often quickly forgot what my illness had ordered me to do. At night it was a completely different story, as I knew I would soon be asleep and potentially not in control. "If you don't do the compulsion (neutralize a bad thought, bully's image) before you go to sleep, you'll sleepwalk and you'll kill someone," the OCD would say. On my therapist's advice, I'd attempt to lie in bed for even just a few minutes and try to not do the compulsion. Still, postponing was incredibly difficult at night, as fatigue would worsen my symptoms and lessen my resolve. As a result, I'd frequently find myself getting back up and going on to ritualize. On occasion I would get lucky and fall asleep while trying to postpone, and then wake up the following morning to see that the fear had faded away. Strangely, this success still failed to convince me that the OCD threat was a bluff. Instead, the same threat would always return the next night and feel even more intense.

Over time, I continued to struggle hard with my OCD. I also had a difficult time staying motivated in college, and often fell far behind in my work. Although community college was my first positive experience in a school setting, I had a perfectionist attitude when it came to my studies. Instead of sticking it out, I would drop all my classes when things got tough and resolve to start over the following semester. As one could imagine, this quickly became a self-destructive pattern for me.

Running from problems seemed to be the approach I was taking in life. This was true most of all when it came to confronting my OCD. Feeling too afraid to take my illness head on, I came up with many creative new ways to get around facing my fears.

CHAPTER NINE
A PHILOSOPHY BASED ON AVOIDANCE

In general, there is nothing unusual about parents pushing their children. Parents typically push their kids in a variety of different ways, often encouraging and guiding them in a positive direction. In the throes of a mental illness, this pushing may take a physical form, such as having to literally shove the sick child just to move from one spot to the next!

Incredibly, this is exactly what occurred during my battle with OCD. Dating back to my senior year of high school, my parents had to physically push me a lot just to help me get through every day. Though this tactic first began as a way to force me to stop ritualizing, it became a dysfunctional practice in a philosophy based on avoidance.

As I explained in earlier chapters, images of bullies and terrible threats greatly worsened my OCD. In fact, these components increased my compulsive behaviors and made them much harder to stop. With the passage of time I came to discover one seemingly helpful trick: it was easy to quit ritualizing if someone would interrupt me in the act. This occurred when a person would suddenly catch me engaged in compulsive behaviors. The embarrassment felt from being noticed like this proved to be a tremendous blessing, and remarkably served to cancel out the demands of the OCD! In other words, getting caught seemed to give me a magical means of regaining my free will and walking away.

This phenomenon also occurred if my parents would physically force me to stop. In order to achieve this goal, they would grab me and pull me away from wherever my symptoms had gotten me stuck (one good example being when my dad had to help me leave the hotel back in March 1997). In these cases it wasn't embarrassment that had helped me get off the hook, but rather having the option to ritualize being taken away from me. If this option was gone or appeared to be gone, I would quickly feel free from the threats.

Wanting to assist me in any possible way, my parents willingly pushed me around and did so at my request. To better achieve my objective, I asked them to be quite forceful with me physically until I felt convinced that I had no control. When I felt reassured that they wouldn't relent, I was able to just let it go. Even after getting help and learning the correct way to beat OCD, being pushed around seemed much easier than challenging my disease. However, our method of cheating the OCD only worked for a period of time. Soon we would all come to understand that I was truly cheating myself. This was so because avoidance, as I had been told many times, only increases one's symptoms! The more that you try to avoid what you fear, the stronger those fears will become.

Sure enough, my bad thoughts and desire to ritualize continued to escalate. As a result, it slowly became more difficult for my parents to hold me back. To combat my growing resistance, I now attempted to use my mom and dad's health as the reason to not ritualize. "Is pushing me hurting your health?" I would ask, hoping to hear them reply that it was. When they gave me the answers I'd coached them to give (telling me that the pushing did affect their health, reminding me of their ages, their physical woes, etc.) that became my new way to let go. However, even this modified form of avoidance became ineffective with time.

In spite of my heavy reliance on others, making it impossible to ritualize was also something I could do on my own. This occurred most often when OCD symptoms centered on objects around me. A good example would be whenever I used a Kleenex to wipe my nose. Upon pulling the tissue out of my nostril, I couldn't resist examining it before I threw it away. If I noticed any traces of redness or blood, I'd immediately have an obsessive bad thought about someone I love being killed! Irrational as it was, I now feared that the tissue was possessed with evil and could cause me to carry out harm. The easiest solution appeared to be to simply flush it down the toilet. This way, the 'contaminated' item was gone for good and the thought would soon fade away.

This quickly became standard procedure whenever I used a Kleenex. Yet flushing each tissue away over time seemed to make the thoughts even worse. Along with the usual death threats, soon came the emergence of negative imagery. I was also overwhelmed by very basic doubts about what I had seen on the tissue. Did I see a speck of blood or was it just my imagination? Not feeling sure about what I had seen made me question my mental well-being. To counter this terrible feeling, I'd ritualize by rechecking each piece of tissue over and over for any trace of mucus or marks. But as long as the item remained in the house, my doubts would continue to grow. Only once it was flushed and could not be retrieved would I regain my peace of mind.

As you can probably guess by now, this form of avoidance/cheating only made my symptoms get worse. Before long, I was also experiencing similar issues while wiping my bottom when using the toilet, although these were much more focused on my obsessive need to feel clean. Nonetheless, it led me to fill up the toilet with tissues and cause it to overflow! Tragically, this became a common occurrence for an extended period of time. In fact, I could easily finish a whole roll of toilet paper with just one trip to the pot.

The madness didn't stop there. Over time, many common household items would also end up being flushed away. Take, for example, a tasty bag of microwave popcorn. Oh how I loved my microwave popcorn! As I'd poured the cooked contents into a bowl, my eyes couldn't help but catch a glimpse inside of the empty bag. Almost immediately, a host of tricky obsessive doubts would flood right into my overworked brain (Did I just see an extra piece of popcorn in there? Was that a light yellow stain I saw in that one particular corner of the bag? Did I see a certain number of brown seeds in the bag? etc.). To try to reduce my distress, I'd ritualize by rechecking the inside of the popcorn bag. However, upon doing so, the threats and negative imagery would quickly materialize (typically an image of a bully along with the irrational doubt that if I didn't feel sure about what I'd seen in the bag, then perhaps I also cannot feel sure that the image won't make me do harm). It was a cruel, sadistic, torturous game at which I just couldn't succeed. Rather than live with the doubts, I'd instead cut the used popcorn bag into pieces and flush them all down the toilet. This also occurred many times when I was writing with paper and pen. While completing a random word, I'd suddenly have an obsessive bad thought about stabbing someone with the pen. Like before, I would fear that the paper was 'contaminated' now and could cause me to carry out harm. Therefore, sending it out through the plumbing appeared to be my only escape.

In contrast to the effort it took to flush items down the toilet, avoidance could be as simple as merely choosing to close my eyes. I typically used this defense when faced with doubts about my perceptions. As usual, the time right before I went to sleep was when this occurred most often. It usually began as I attempted to turn off the light in the bathroom and walk to my bed. As I'd reach out to flip the switch, I'd suddenly doubt whether I had just seen a small dark speck on the wall. My uncertainty over this seemingly minor detail was extremely disturbing, and would make me begin to question whether I was losing my mind.

In response, I'd ritualize by turning the light back on and inspecting the wall for marks. These actions only led to further doubts about my perceptions (Examples: Did I just see a hair on that spot of the floor? Was that a sharp object over there on the carpet? Did I see a hanger in a certain spot in the closet? etc.), often accompanied by the emergence of old images and threats. To cheat the ensuing discomfort, I would close my eyes before flipping the switch and then feel my way back to the bed. The relief that I felt once under the sheets was countered with this bitter truth: My avoidance had served to ensure that my symptoms would torment me more the next day, and they did. Over time, I used this form of avoidance during the daytime as well, frequently shutting my eyes as I cautiously moved myself from one room to the next.

In spite of my greatest efforts, I realized that one major thing that I couldn't avoid was the passage of time. By May of 2000, a full three years had elapsed from the moment I finally came clean to my dad. I was 24 years old then and enrolled in community college, but I still hadn't made much significant progress in dealing with OCD. Around this point in time, I decided to tell a trusted professor about my entire ordeal. During our lengthy conversation, I told her about my history of being bullied at school and the impact it had on my life.

In response, my professor helped me uncover yet another strange form of avoidance: blame. So often my OCD brought negative images up from the past, and I'd mistakenly feel I was battling bullies instead of a clever disease! As a result, I'd begin to dwell over things from the past and lose sight of the battles today. To clear this mental confusion, she suggested that I someday track down my worst bully and have a confrontation with him. This way, I could put blaming others behind me and keep myself focused on OCD. In short, it appeared that my philosophy based on avoidance needed to radically change.

CHAPTER TEN

CONFRONTATION WITH A BULLY

Michael Beckert wasn't really bigger or stronger than me physically. In fact, he was slightly shorter and heavyset. Not overly threatening at a first glance, but what he lacked in overall size and strength he made up with intimidation. Unlike many who had bullied me, including some of his closest friends, Michael displayed more aggressiveness and wouldn't back down even when I stood up for myself. He and I had a history dating back to elementary school, and he clearly relished picking on me relentlessly over the years. Tragically, the impact of Michael's harassment, long after it had ended, was given a brand new life by my OCD. As fate would cruelly dictate, the image of this bully's menacing face would torture me in ways I could have never conceived.

The earliest incident I remember with Michael was of him and his buddies kicking the bathroom stall door in my face and yelling, "Sumi's on the pot! Sumi's on the pot!" Over time, physical aggression by Michael towards me became a common occurrence. I vividly recall one such incident in elementary school gym class, when Michael called out my name and then threw a basketball hard, right into my face! He was kind enough to then take a moment and chuckle at the accuracy of his good aim. Michael was also a part of the group that liked to make fun of my ethnic background. In addition to mocking my first, middle, and last name, Michael made negative comments about my skin color and where I originally came from.

Aside from all he did to me at school, Michael and his crew were brazen enough to even harass my parents! In the fifth or sixth grade, I remember my family being awakened in the middle of the night by numerous prank phone calls. I later found out from others at school that Michael had been the ringleader in this. There was also a time when I ran into Michael and his boys while bike riding home from a friend's house with my dad. Apparently unfazed by the presence of my father, the three eagerly peddled fast after us, yelling out taunting remarks.

Out of all the abuse I endured from Michael, one incident in particular came to eerily resemble the future threats of my OCD. During my sixth grade year in middle school, Michael and a friend once cornered me inside the boys' bathroom. Standing guard at the entrance, Michael ordered me to lick my finger and use it to rub away a mark on a urinal. If I refused to do so, the boys had vowed they would both beat me up. Regrettably, I took the smug jerks at their word and did what they told me to do. Also, later during my sixth grade year, Michael and his pals surrounded and harassed me intensely inside the boys' gym locker room. As I was attempting to change outfits, Michael and the guys began pulling my clothes and other items from me and throwing them all over the locker room. This was done in front of numerous other students, as the three or four of them laughed and kept on calling out my name with tremendous enjoyment.

As horrible as these previous incidents were, there was still more to come from Michael. In my seventh grade year at middle school, the bullying got even worse. Along with shoving me into my locker and striking me hard with a rubber band, Michael boldly challenged me to fight him on "the hill" after school. This "hill" was an infamous spot where feuding kids went to settle the score. Too frightened to face my opponent, my dad and I went to the school counselor and he finally got Michael to stop. Still, this change wasn't immediate. Instead, Michael taunted me now for being afraid and reporting him to the school.

Over the next few months, I had even further encounters with Michael. One Friday night, a couple of months later, I ran into Michael and his friends at a local arcade. Being there with my dad and my brother, the boys kept their hands to themselves. Instead, they verbally taunted us from a safe distance and shot rubber bands at our backs. Apparently Michael still wasn't fully satisfied with his work. On the last day of school before winter break that year, Michael suddenly punched me hard in the chest as he and a buddy chuckled and scurried down the hallway.

In the next few years, Michael appeared to naturally mature somewhat and didn't harass me again. In fact, after freshman year of high school, Michael transferred to a different school and was no longer around. However, knowing that Michael wasn't there didn't help to ease my pain and regret. For years to come I would long for revenge and despise myself for not taking him on.

Tragic as all this was, for someone not cursed with OCD, this is where the ordeal would end. Not so in my case, however. Because once images of bullies from my past came to be part of my OCD symptom pattern, Michael's image was the most common one of them all! It was like I'd been sentenced to picture this asshole's menacing face everywhere for the rest of my life! Each of the countless times that this occurred on a single given day, I wondered if fighting Michael as a kid could have simply prevented it all.

While that issue may be up for debate, my emotional state was not. Over time, it had become harder for me to fight my illness and not be consumed with anger. By May of 2000, I found myself unable to separate Michael from my OCD. In my mind Michael literally *was* my disease, as it most often used his image along with a hideous threat to torment and control me. Therefore, it seemed that, in order to face OCD, I'd first have to face Michael Beckert. In other words, I'd have to track down my very worst bully from school and have a confrontation with him!

On the surface, the very idea seemed absurd, not to mention difficult to facilitate, and potentially dangerous. After all, Michael had not been a nice person! In fact, after graduating high school, my dad and I saw Michael on the local news in a story about teen smokers. One portion of the segment showed Michael smoking a cigarette on camera, sporting long hair and a rough appearance that made him look, in my dad's opinion, like a "jailbird." This random sighting of Michael had occurred nearly five years earlier, back in August 1995. In reality, I hadn't had contact with Michael for nearly the past eight years. I had no clue as to what his personality was like, or if he even still lived in Minnesota.

Besides, could I really come face to face with Michael without wanting to rip him apart? What would I even say to him? "Hey, dude, your smirking face tortures me everyday and you totally ruined my life?" If he was still an asshole, did I want to give him the satisfaction and power of knowing the extent of the harm he had caused? It seemed such a confrontation might not be beneficial to me. After much discussion with my parents, my therapist, and a trusted college professor, I decided this was something that I simply had to do.

Fortunately, finding Michael's parents' home phone number wasn't a difficult process. As it turned out, his family lived just minutes away from where I still lived with my parents. Finally, on Tuesday, May 30, 2000, it was time to make the call. With adrenalin racing through me, I picked up the phone, dialed the number, and held my breath for an answer.

"Hello," came the reply on the other side from a male voice.

"Yes, hello," I responded. "I was wondering if I could speak to Michael please?" I proceeded to inquire. To my great surprise, the male voice responded by saying, "Yes, this is him."

After confirming that I was speaking to the right person, I simply stated, "Hey, Michael, it's me, Sumi."

Michael remembered me instantly, and quickly responded by saying, "You mean you're Sumi Mukherjee?"

"Yes, I am," I replied. I then went on to tell Michael that I wanted to meet with him to discuss things that had happened between us in the past at school.

"What kind of things?" he cautiously asked me.

I told him I wanted to discuss how he had bullied me and the long-term impact it had on my life. Without acknowledging any guilt, he said he remembered being in the same section with me in elementary school and recalled "harassment happening between us." Remarkably, he was also still living with his parents and said he'd be willing to meet with me. We agreed to meet at a Perkins restaurant at 2 p.m. on Saturday, June 3. Then, strangely, Michael wished me well and thanked me for calling before hanging up the phone.

Later that evening, I called my best friend, Kyle, and had him come over. For the first time ever, I told Kyle all about having OCD and trying to confront Michael Beckert. To date, Kyle was the only friend from high school whom I hadn't lost contact with. For years I had been concerned that if he didn't understand my illness, then I could end up losing the best friend I ever had. Luckily, Kyle was full of compassion and understanding, and himself recalled Michael Beckert as being a typical bully. In fact, he applauded my courage and said calling Michael had been a big step for me. We also decided that if I still wanted to fight him, I could challenge Michael to have a boxing match after the confrontation! Kyle came up with the idea after seeing this concept played out in a television show, where people who didn't like one another put on some gloves and had it out. Crazy as this all sounded, I felt completely elated. It appeared that I would finally get the chance for some closure and justice.

Maybe so, but it wouldn't come easy. On Saturday, June 3, I was pumped up for a dramatic confrontation. In spite of being plenty nervous, I showed up at the restaurant just as we had planned. The only problem was that, for whatever reason, Michael Beckert did *not* show up! Yet the emotional roller coaster ride was just beginning. When returning home from a family outing later that evening, I found a very kind, maturely worded message from Michael on the answering machine. In the message, he apologized deeply for not showing up and said that he wanted to reschedule a meeting. However, when I called him back the following day, Michael had suddenly changed his mind. After apologizing again for his failure to show up, Michael now stated that he didn't want to meet. "This is all negative stuff that you want to talk about," he told me in a strange, robotic tone of voice. "I don't see much point in talking about bad things that are in the past."

Accepting his refusal to meet, I told Michael there was something that he needed to hear from me. Speaking out strongly, I summarized to him how much he had hurt me and how I had felt so weak and afraid. I concluded by saying I was no longer scared and that he needed to understand the impact of his actions. Surprisingly, Michael patiently listened throughout my whole speech. At the conclusion, he replied by simply saying "thank you" in the same robotic tone as I angrily hung up the phone. In spite of my frustration and deep disappointment, at least I'd expressed my emotions to Michael, and that would have to suffice. Or would it? Stunningly, just one hour later, Michael called me yet again! This time, he said he was open to having our meeting and that I should call with a date and time.

Over the next few days Michael and I played phone tag until we finally connected. At this point, we agreed to meet on Friday at the restaurant for dinner. This time, he insisted, he was going to show up.

As it turned out, he sure did. On Friday, June 9, 2000, I came face to face with my absolute worst bully of all time. Tense, but also ready, I walked in the restaurant at 6 p.m. and saw Michael sitting there on a bench. He immediately met my eyes and rose as if summoned by someone to do so. We said hi, shook hands, and the restaurant greeter smiled and told me, "He's been waiting here awhile to see you."

Interestingly, Michael hadn't changed much in appearance. He was a little shorter than me, and more heavyset, just as he had been back in school. Only now the long hair from that 1995 newscast was gone and he looked like an altar boy. Upon being seated and given menus, Michael and I placed our orders and slowly began to talk.

I started by asking Michael what made him finally decide to meet with me after so much hesitation. Impressively, he explained that my speech to him over the phone had made quite an impact on him. "I realized that you had been hurt, and I thought that coming here could lead to some healing and forgiveness," he said in response to my question. Following my therapist's advice, I decided not to tell Michael about my having OCD. I felt he didn't need to know about my crippling mental illness and about his personal "image" being stuck in my tortured brain. Instead, I asked him what he remembered about our past together as classmates.

I had been well prepared by now for him to be somewhat defensive, or to try to deny or diminish all of the things he had done. Surprisingly, Michael had just the opposite reaction to my questions. "I remember picking on you a lot in elementary school, prank phone calling your house at night," he candidly admitted. Incredibly, Michael even recalled the exact words he had said on the night, now some 13 years ago, when he had made those prank calls to my house! During this conversation, Michael also proceeded to apologize directly for all that he had put me through.

As we continued to talk, I got to learn more about what was going on in Michael's life. Ironic as it seemed, he now claimed to be a born-again Christian, and said his life revolved around his family, work, and the church. Michael also shared revealing things about his past with me. He talked about a somewhat troubled childhood, his mother's horrible temper, his parents' difficult divorce, and being picked on at times by his older brother. "I think those are the things that poisoned my life," Michael stated, "and in turn, I believe I poisoned the lives of others around me."

Something that struck me as odd throughout our meeting was Michael's way of speaking and his mannerisms in general. Of course it seemed unreal to be having a mature conversation with him, but the strangeness I was observing went even further than that. There appeared to be a clear, almost zombie-like slowness in Michael's demeanor. His movements seemed sluggish in an unnatural kind of way. Though I couldn't really put my finger on it, something clearly didn't seem right. Kyle had even noticed this when listening to a voice message Michael had left me. "It's kinda strange how he speaks, how he pronounces his words," Kyle had told me. Regardless of what was behind all this, we carried on with our discussion.

One by one, I went through my written list of several incidents in which Michael bullied me as a kid. Contrary to what my therapist anticipated, Michael freely admitted to everything, including things I recalled that he couldn't even remember. "If you remember me doing that to you, then I'm sure I must have done it," Michael candidly stated. "I used to have a really smart mouth, and people have given me feedback, including someone recently at my work, that I sometimes say and do very insensitive things." To balance against his generous apologies and confessions, there was one thing Michael kept doing that night which made me question his sincerity. As I recalled each traumatic bullying incident from the past, a mischievous naughty grin would slowly spread widely across Michael's face. It was the exact same smirk that had haunted me through my OCD for all of these many years; it was the same evil look he had on his face when he had been tormenting me. It was almost as if now, even all these many years later, Michael was still deriving some cruel satisfaction from reliving the things he had done. It was more than someone just smiling with embarrassment over regrettable acts in his youth. Rather, Michael appeared to be beaming and glowing, as though we were recalling his fondest childhood memories! Along with grinning widely and smirking, Michael even slipped a time or two, and referred to some of his group's cruel acts as being funny. Having said so, Michael then quickly corrected himself and asserted that what he did had *not* actually been funny, given the fact that it was done at my expense.

By the end of our meal and discussion, I felt I'd achieved my objective, with the exception of one little thing. As we prepared to pay for dinner, I casually told Michael about the television program in which people had boxing matches to settle their differences. I then reminded him of his challenge to "fight on the hill" back in middle school in the seventh grade, and how I'd been too afraid back then to actually do it. "I need to look you in the eyes and say that I'm not scared of you," I bravely told Michael as he acknowledged me and nodded. Pausing briefly for a moment, I then continued by saying, "Furthermore, I now would like to accept your offer from the seventh grade and hereby challenge you to have a boxing match with me!"

MICHAEL WAS SPEECHLESS. He just sat there with a completely dumbfounded look across his face. Eventually, he looked up at me and cautiously inquired, "So... you're challenging me???" I held his gaze and wore a slight smile now, seeing that his smirk was long gone.

"Yeah Michael, I am," I replied. He proceeded to ask this same question a second time and again I confirmed that yes I was indeed challenging him. At this point, Michael appeared even more confused, and shook his head as if stumped by my answer.

"Ummmmmmmm, I don't know, I'll have to think about it," he finally managed to utter in a dazed, emotionless tone.

Up until this point in the evening, Michael had conversed with me freely and in a seemingly normal manner. From this particular point onwards, Michael suddenly seemed unable to speak or communicate with me any further. He just sat there strangely for several minutes, almost appearing to be in some sort of a trance. Eventually, Michael managed to slowly make his way out of the restaurant and all the way back to his car. Although he held the restaurant door open for me, shook my hand in the parking lot, and made an odd hand gesture towards me, Michael did not utter a single word as our interactions strangely concluded.

As it turned out in the end, there was never a boxing match. Michael called me a few days after we met and declined my invitation to step into the ring. I told him that was all right with me, but to know that my offer still stands. I also gave Michael a letter, thanking him for acknowledging all he had done wrong, and for finally attempting to change the ways in which he treats other people.

While this unique event didn't change the frequency of Michael's image in my OCD, a lot of good things did happen as a result of the confrontation. Shortly after our meeting in June, I started to work out again, initially to get myself back into shape in case Michael someday would want to fight. With time, my old passion for physical fitness re-emerged, and I was finally able to exercise *without* the obsessive perfection. This was certainly a wonderful achievement for me, as I hadn't worked out because of my illness for nearly the past seven years!

There was another truly amazing, tremendous gift that I had gained from confronting Michael. For many years I'd have terrible nightmares where Michael and his friends were relentlessly tormenting me, and I'd wake up feeling victimized all over again. After the June 2000 confrontation, my dreams had dramatically changed. In my new dreams over the following decade, Michael would now be kind and respectful to me and would rarely cause me any trouble! In fact, he would often appear physically much smaller and weaker in my dreams than he had actually been in real life. I even found myself having dreams where some of Michael's friends would harass me, but Michael alone would politely refrain. I'm so grateful for how empowering this specific change has been in my life!

As a result of these positive things I was also now fighting my OCD better. However, trying to rebuild my once shattered life would still be a difficult task.

Update 2010: While surfing the internet on Google in early June of that year, I was stunned to come across Michael Beckert's obituary in a major Minneapolis newspaper, identifying him as having passed away two years ago at the age of 31. Along with a photograph of him that I recognized, the comments mentioned that Michael had died "as a result of his long-term illness of Schizophrenia." I could hardly believe the one bully who contributed most to my mental illness, had incredibly suffered an even worse mental illness of his own!

I found it quite ironic that in the five years preceding my proper OCD diagnosis in 1997, I myself had lived with the paralyzing fear that perhaps I was schizophrenic! Most ironic of all, is the fact that Michael's funeral took place at a church in St. Paul, MN, which was located on a street with the name of 'Summit Ave', which is almost exactly the same spelling as my full first name, Sumit. Either way, it is the name that Michael Beckert had mocked so thoroughly during his shortened life.

With more research, I came to learn that Michael had suffered a devastating onset of Schizo-Affective Disorder in 1996 at the age of 19. I learned there had been a history of the illness in Michael's family, and an uncle on his mother's side had also suffered from Schizophrenia. I was able to further confirm that Michael's tragic death in August 2008 had been self-inflicted, and occurred after Michael had struggled for twelve long years with his awful disease. In retrospect, this insight now serves to finally explain what may have been going on inside Michael's mind when I had challenged him to have a boxing match, on Friday, June 9, 2000. He may have simply had a difficult time in processing this information, or it may have even triggered an episode of hearing voices inside of his head.

In all honesty, the stunning news of Michael's untimely death had left me with mixed emotions. In spite of the negative history between us, I did, and do in fact feel compassion for Michael. I had even felt compassion when I met him at the Perkins restaurant in June of 2000, when he had been 23 years old and four years into his illness. I'd observed back then that Michael didn't look altogether so well, although I had been unaware until now of the shocking reason why. Knowing now, everything else seems to fall into place. This explains why the older Michael spoke in a flat and emotionless tone, and why he said some of his words in a seemingly strange and unusual way.

Being only human, I have also felt emotions of a less compassionate nature concerning what happened to Michael. I felt guilty for feeling this way, but have tried not to blame myself for being human. Our feelings, at any given moment, do not have to define who we are overall. Thoughts do not equal actions, and as complex human beings we can often feel many conflicting things at the same time. I have always been a hard-core believer in karma, retribution, and justice, and often feel as though such factors may have indeed been at play. While I do not feel as though I can forgive the cruel kid who had tormented me without pause, I do feel some forgiveness for the born-again Christian who acknowledged the wrongs he had done, particularly when considering his own deterioration. Lots of people do horrible things in life and never apologize, never admit to their flaws, and never own up to their actions. It helped me greatly to receive a full apology from Michael, along with his validation of what I had endured. Although I cannot measure Michael's sincerity in deciding to meet up with me, I do know that the meeting has changed my life and will always be grateful for that.

It is, of course, most ironic, as I mentioned before, that Michael and I have both faced the burdens that come with being mentally ill. At our meeting, I had previously decided to conceal my mental health issues from Michael. I never could have imagined, not even in a million years, that Michael was concealing something similar from me! In the end, Michael Beckert had transformed into the same kind of person whom he had once loved to torment; a weaker, less fortunate, troubled young man who just couldn't find peace in life. A huge, important lesson which I have taken from all this, is the wisdom that things in life may not always be just as they appear. For so many years I imagined that Michael was prospering while I was crippled, and that all of the people who tormented me must be getting much more out of life.

The remarkable, highly ironic true story of Michael Beckert shows me that this may not be the case. Those who we envy and feel jealous of may have problems that we'll never know.

Perhaps it is true, what I've heard all along, that the best revenge is a good life.

CHAPTER ELEVEN
STRUGGLING TO COPE
WITH THE LOST YEARS

"Your past is in the past. Your next 60-70 years is completely the future you choose to make." - Dad

It seemed many things came together for me soon after confronting Michael Beckert. As predicted, standing up to my bully did help me refocus my efforts against OCD. Exercise also proved to be another fantastic achievement. In fact, in the next twelve months I eventually went onto lose about 50 pounds, going from a pants size 42 way down to a 34! Having grown tired of college, I obtained yet another hospitality job in March of 2002. I began, at the late age of 25, to think about dating at last. For the very first time since the age of sixteen, I was starting to live once again. Ironically, improvements in life also helped me to see how much time I had let slip away.

In other words, struggling to cope with the lost years became a major issue for me. The toughest part, I believe, was realizing how much I still hadn't done in comparison to many other people my age. Though my life had been interrupted now for almost ten years, there's a world out there full of people who have made progress in their own lives. The educations, careers, and relationships of others were never frozen in time or put on hold as they had long been for me.

Yes folks, it's hard being an American man in his mid-upper twenties who was still a virgin, still living with his parents and financially dependent on them. While I slowly began to make changes in all of these various areas, my journey back to the present time hasn't been quick or easy. On the contrary, the loss of teenage years and early adulthood took quite a toll on my life. As a result, I've been left with a strong sense of urgency that accompanies all that I do.

While this urgency encompasses a wide range of life experiences, it has most dominantly been centered on the concept of having fun. Feeling like I've missed the more enjoyable aspects of youth, I went out of my way to try to somehow re-capture my teenage years! This strange endeavor led me to a lifestyle of partying, alcohol use, and sexual promiscuity. Not to mention excessive risk taking.

Soon, behaviors I once envied and despised in others became quite appealing to me. After years of being a slave to the rigid rules of a brutal disease, it felt great to be irresponsible and not have a care in the world!

Though having a good time on the surface my life, overall, remained empty and unfulfilling. In addition to first being bullied and then developing OCD, my third major phase of misfortune came in dealing with the opposite sex. Only now beginning to date, I experienced a whole lot of heartache and very bad luck with girls. Much like throughout school, my ethnicity in Minnesota appeared to make dating much tougher for me. Over time, these setbacks affected me deeply and left me extremely depressed. They also created an overwhelming, long-term sense of hopelessness and pessimism. With the pressure of the lost years weighing on my shoulders, I found myself growing more afraid that time was running out.

To this day I struggle immensely with the impact from the lost years. However, I am also aware that my future still offers promise and potential. The decision to let go of my past is one I am quite capable of making. Yes it's true I've lost many years, but there are many more good years to live; that is, assuming I don't make foolish mistakes which would force me to start from scratch...

CHAPTER TWELVE
A DEVASTATING RELAPSE

"Perhaps the most brutally accurate way to measure that which you have gained is through the painful process of losing it again."

Drinking alcohol while on medication for a mental illness can be an interesting experience. On what may seem like the positive side, the "high" from intoxication can last well into the following day. On the negative side, the hangover symptoms from a wild night of drinking can linger for as long as a week. Such symptoms can include headaches, upset stomach, and feeling lethargic. Each person who chooses to drink while on meds may experience something different. Regardless, the fact remains that alcohol and medication just don't mix well together. As time went on, I felt I had to choose one over the other. Not about to sacrifice my new partying lifestyle, I decided against my doctor's advice to go off my medications!

Over time, this proved to be an extremely poor choice for which I would pay an immeasurable price. Zoloft and Seroquel, the meds I was on at the time, are drugs that are not designed to be stopped all at once. Rather, when going off them, one must do so gradually, a little bit at a time, and with a professional's guidance. However, in my haste to consume more alcohol without bad after effects, I abandoned my better judgment and simply quit taking my meds cold turkey.

Once again, it was great to break the same old rules that had governed my life for so long. Believing I no longer needed medication seemed to be another feather in my cap. So, too, was finally moving into my own place, a townhouse unit that my parents owned and rented out to me. Between hotel jobs, having fun, and taking college classes, I also took time to mentor a deeply troubled nine-year-old boy. He was the son of a former co-worker and close friend of mine, and my influence in his life seemed to be making a world of difference. By all accounts, it looked as though I was able to make things work.

While it felt like my OCD may have disappeared, it had merely changed appearance and method of attack. Though I'd been fairly free from old rituals and threats of unspeakable harm, different bad thoughts and obsessive concerns had taken their place instead. Such doubts often centered on my health, the things I enjoyed about life, and my perception of specific events. I also questioned my morality and intellect in various life situations. Still, these symptoms seemed far better than the rituals of the past, which I knew could incapacitate me from functioning much at all. If I thought that I'd evolved beyond those most dreadful days, I was in for an ugly surprise.

By December 2004, it was all catching up to me. Going off my meds had finally come back to blow up in my face. Soon, I found myself performing rituals again and fearing disturbing threats. Only now, the threats had changed a bit in their nature. Instead of suggesting that I might kill my family, (which was so far fetched by now I felt quite certain it wouldn't happen), my illness handed out threats on a seemingly more realistic level.

Or at least that is how it felt. The most awful example of this occurred when I was caring for a friend's pet bunny. It started out as a peaceful evening, watching reruns on Nick-at -Nite with the furry little creature against my chest. As my hand gently caressed her back, I suddenly pictured the image of a bully. There was also an immediate doubt as to whether a certain part of my fingers had brushed against a specific part of her fur.

Disturbed by this image and doubt, I ran my fingers through her fur again, hoping to ease these troubling feelings. Upon doing so, I had another even more unsettling thought; a threat that if I didn't rub her back in the same spot again, but with a little more pressure, I would lose control and begin striking her! Fearing the threat, I continued to rub her back, obeying the OCD and pressing down on her more with my fingers. Yet each time I did so the threat just grew stronger, compelling me as usual to continue the ritual.

Soon this escalated from just rubbing the bunny to patting her back with my hand repeatedly, with more pressure and force than I would ordinarily use. *"Aha!"* screamed the OCD, zeroing in on my weakness. "You're hitting the bunny! I can make you hit this helpless creature and you can't stop yourself! See, you CAN'T stop. If I can make you pat her harder than you'd like, what else can I make you do? How much further can I talk you into doing?" The harder I tried to stop, the stronger this threat became. "If you stop patting her now, you'll lose control later and return to strike her hard!" my illness kept saying. While continuing the ritual appeared to be a way to prevent potential harm to the bunny, I also felt it was proof that the OCD could indeed control my actions. Either way, I was damned if I stopped the ritual and damned if I didn't. Caught between a rock and a hard place, it seemed there was no way out.

As the minutes rolled on, I continued carrying out the ritual. With each passing moment, I felt I was closer to harming this innocent life with whose care I'd been trusted. "You're alone in the house, what's to stop you from hitting this bunny harder and harder until she's dead?" the OCD tauntingly asked me. "You know deep down inside you want to kill her. You always have. Well tonight's the night. TONIGHT'S THE NIGHT AFTER ALL THESE YEARS THAT I'LL FINALLY FORCE YOU TO KILL!!!"

Once again my brilliant enemy had manipulated my thinking. Instead of the outright death threats I'd grown accustomed to, the OCD had started me at a much lower level. By giving in to that smaller fear, I had bitten the hook and taken the bait. Once I was trapped in this ritual, the death threats quickly returned. As I continued patting the bunny on her back I keenly observed her face, searching for any hint of anguish or discomfort. In sharp contrast to me she was pretty calm, and even seemed relaxed at times. *Oh good,* I thought to myself. *If she looks content, then I can't possibly be hurting her...or could I still be???*

Sadly, this ritual continued all night until about 6 in the morning. To survive the prolonged torture, I managed to take periodic breaks and even had a friend come over. Over several hours I was able to move across the room and put the bunny back in her cage. Even having done so, I was still unable to stop performing the ritual. This time, it seemed, I had gone too far and there was just no turning back. At one point I became dizzy and thought I might pass out, as a wave of tension surged from my chest up to my head.

Eventually, physical exhaustion overwhelmed me and I was somehow able to stop. As I collapsed on the couch to finally sleep I was sweaty and dehydrated. Worst of all, I had completely lost all confidence in fighting the OCD. The incident reinforced the false belief that my illness could control my actions, and that refusing to complete a ritual may produce harmful or deadly results.

Over the next couple of months, I became more unable to function with each passing day. It was reminiscent of those most awful times in March 1997; only this time around it felt even worse. Too afraid to challenge my illness, I found myself ritualizing almost all the time. For example, I was no longer able to speak normally. Instead, I'd feel compelled to repeat certain words several times to ward off terrible threats. I also found myself asking my lady friend to repeat certain trivial things, such as her own words and actions upon which I felt an OCD threat.

Soon, my friend and her son began staying with me for support, as I required constant assistance to complete even the most basic tasks. These included eating, using the bathroom and getting myself to bed... or for that matter, any other daily activity you can possibly name! Without someone there to coach me and to physically push me along, I found it nearly impossible for me to get through each day.

Over time we knew that we couldn't go on like this, as the lifestyle wasn't healthy for any of us. In fact, it was counterproductive towards the goal of someday regaining control of my life. Something major had to be done and it needed to happen fast! By March 2005, I was willing to try anything. It was at this point that my therapist recommended a high intensity, inpatient residential treatment program designed for those with the worst OCD. The program was run at Rogers Memorial Hospital in Oconomowoc, Wisconsin. It was just one of three places in the country that could facilitate such a program. The average stay for a patient was between 45 to 60 days, although a guy who I knew from group therapy ended up there for four months! With a cost of about $500 per day, most patients relied on insurance to cover this major expense. At any rate, there was no guarantee that I could even get in soon, as there was usually a lengthy waiting list many months long.

Surprisingly, upon calling the hospital I found that they had availability the very next month! This was truly a huge break for me, as I obviously couldn't go on without treatment. At long last, it seemed like I had found the right solution for my troubles, and this program was the miracle remedy that would finally set me free...

CHAPTER THIRTEEN

JOURNEY TO THE PROMISED LAND

"Sometimes in life it helps to view success as an ongoing journey rather than a final destination."

The drive to Oconomowoc, Wisconsin from my home in Minnesota can take anywhere between five to six hours, mostly depending on whether you speed and how often you stop to use the restroom. For me, it had been a 13-year journey through the depths of hell to finally get to this point. That overwhelming sense of urgency was fresh in my mind on Wednesday, April 13, 2005, as I pulled up the scenic entrance to Rogers Memorial Hospital at 1:34p.m. Only this time, I realized, I wouldn't be going home.

I had driven up and toured the facility with family and friends just two days earlier, at which time staff informed me of a bed being available Wednesday night. It was quite a shock for us all, as we'd predicted I would likely wait another week and a half before I could be admitted. I also had the honor of meeting a very incredible young lady that same afternoon. Megan, as I will call her, was a thirteen-year-old girl suffering from OCD. She had come to Rogers with her parents, just as I had, as a last resort. Though young Megan was merely half my age, she had already endured being misdiagnosed repeatedly, being improperly hospitalized through error, and being made to endure four long years of terrible hardship.

From the moment I first saw Megan I immediately *knew* that she had OCD! I could see it right away in her walking, how she took such carefully timed, precise steps with her feet. The fact that she nearly freaked out when she saw a nearby sink (presumably related to hand washing/contamination fears) provided me with another good clue! I guess the old saying is true that it takes one to know one. One of my friends picked up on it, too, and was kind enough to help Megan spit out her chewing gum into a garbage can, a process which appeared to present quite a struggle for her.

What really moved me about Megan was how petrified she looked when she entered the hospital lobby, along with the tired looks of anguish on the faces of her parents. This scenario was all too familiar to me, and it was difficult to now watch another family go through it. After speaking to her parents, I calmly approached the girl and said, "Hi, Megan. My name is Sumi and I have had OCD for thirteen years. I just wanted to let you know that you've already made one new friend here." As I said these words and shook her trembling little hand, she smiled at me nervously but appeared to be more at ease. I also gave her father a hug and wished them all the very best. By the time we walked out of the lobby, I was nearly in tears. Seeing what OCD had put this family through hit me just a little too close to home.

As the reality of my impending departure began to sink in, we made the somber trip back to Minnesota that evening and planned a farewell party for the following day. It was truly a blessing to have so many friends in my corner, especially after all of my seemingly endless years of social isolation. While some at the gathering became emotional and even shed tears (We anticipated I'd be gone for about two months), I didn't start to feel the impact of my situation until after I arrived at Rogers.

Although the ride on Wednesday had been somewhat stressful, it certainly paled in comparison to the struggle of leaving my house that morning! Even as my dad drove into the hospital's main entrance, I was busy performing my usual rituals in the backseat of his car. To be honest, I felt like an alcoholic drinking and driving on my way into rehab! The obsessive fears of killing hadn't magically vanished upon my arrival here at what I considered to be the 'Promised Land,' and I continued to perform my rituals in the bathroom on the first floor. The worst of it didn't hit me until I sat down with the intake person to do my paperwork. It was at a moment then that my concerns came full circle and I suddenly thought to myself, WHAT IF THIS OCD TREATMENT PROGRAM JUST DOESN'T HELP ME AT ALL??? What would be my next move for getting further help or treatment? After all, this place was known as the best of the best, the end of the road for the worst OCDers, and what possible options would I have left if the program didn't work out for me?

The only solution I could immediately think of was the high-risk brain surgery, which is not at all guaranteed and filled with serious long-term complications. My friend Rob from our OCD group in Minnesota had almost gone ahead and done it, that is until he spent four months at Rogers and left there feeling 70 percent better off.

Rob's OCD case was even worse than mine, which left me with this troubling thought: If the program here at Rogers doesn't help me at all, then what have I got left to try???

After completing the necessary paperwork for admittance, my dad and I left the main hospital building and drove a short distance to the nearby Lake Houses (Lake House #3 and #4), one of which would be my new home. The lake homes at Rogers that house OCD patients are vastly different from the neighboring buildings on the property, some of which include programs for children and teens (including the children's OCD program located in the main hospital where my friend Megan was staying), eating disorders, and drug/alcohol addictions. Rather than resembling the traditional hospital setting, Lake Houses 3 and 4 are set up as residential homes, the intent being to replicate the patient's typical home environment to better combat their daily symptoms. Nestled snugly near the woods with a gorgeous view of the lake, they could easily pass for your typical summer cabins. It is on the inside of these homes, however, where the loss of your freedom is felt.

At least that is how it felt to me. Upon arriving and being assigned to a room in Lake House 3, my dad and I began the process of bringing my luggage up into the bedroom. Before I could settle in, one of the RCs (Residential Counselors) on duty that afternoon informed us that she had to go through all of my belongings as part of their routine inspection. Helen, as I will call her, was apparently not having a very good day. Her allergies were acting up big time, and she was complaining about them as she went through my luggage. Finding it hard to resist, I jokingly made her an impossible offer. "You wanna trade your allergies for my OCD?"

Smiling slightly, she paused for a moment and responded by saying, "Ahhh no. I won't take you up on that one."

Although I was trying to joke around, on the inside I was beginning to feel really crummy. Having someone sort through my stuff was bothering me more than I would have imagined. It made me feel like an inmate at a prison, as though I no longer had the basic trust given an adult. This feeling only intensified when Helen confiscated several items I had brought, including among other things my cool mint Listerine bottle, a bag of shaving razors, a beard trimmer, and a small bottle of cologne. "Why does the cologne have to go?" I pleaded, almost laughing a bit with amazement.

"Well, it has alcohol in it, just like the Listerine does," she replied. "One time a lady here drank a whole bottle of perfume just for the alcohol, so this has become our standard procedure." I would still have access to my items, she explained, but would have to go to the downstairs office and specifically request to use them as needed. When I was finished, I'd have to bring them back down to the office, where they'd remain locked up in a closet.

The one positive thing at the time was the fact that I'd have the whole room to myself. While most patients had to have roommates, the only person they could've paired me with would have been a woman. "Obviously, we're not going to have you room with a female," chuckled Lorie, another RC on duty.

Now, had my mood been better I would have been all over this one with smart responses like, "Well I wouldn't complain about it," or "I have an obsessive fear of women, no really I do, especially the attractive ones, they terrify me... and it's time that I face my fears to the fullest!" However, the way I was feeling at that moment, I was just grateful to have my own room.

As that first day at Rogers slowly dragged on, my mood only continued to deteriorate. I was quiet and withdrawn when introduced to the whole group of patients in Lake House 4, which is where residents from both houses gather to eat dinner. I just didn't get it. I had come here expecting to feel upbeat and positive and ready to take back my life. Instead, I was feeling worried, depressed, and disappointed in myself. Perhaps the experience was triggering memories of my first days at school, or of how for so many years my greatest fear was to be at a place like this. At any rate, it was strange being shuffled from one doctor to another as part of the intake process. I also felt humiliated when I went out the second night with a group on my first 'belongings run'. As we walked into a Wal-Mart to do our shopping, Mary, the RC on duty, told me discretely not to stray far from her side. "You're new and still under supervision for the first week," she leaned in to tell me. "So just make sure that you stay where I can see you at all times." In that one moment I felt my 28-year old self being transformed back into a five-year-old child! If I thought that life at Rogers was difficult now, I hadn't seen anything yet.

Meeting my housemates, it turned out, would in itself be a challenge! There were three fellow patients besides myself also residing in Lake House 3. Betty, as I will call her, was a wife and mother who had traveled a long distance to Wisconsin for her treatment. Unlike many at Rogers, Betty did not have the luxury of hiding her symptoms from the view of others. Plagued by obsessive fears of germs and contamination, she refused to even shake my hand the day that I met her! That was just the tip of the iceberg for Betty. Aside from handshaking, she would have a panic attack if someone stood or sat slightly close to where she was. She rarely, if ever, went on the weekly group outings (typically 'belongings runs' on Tuesdays and Thursdays and a fun activity on either Saturday or Sunday) and would barricade herself in her room when we returned, to keep safe from whatever "outside germs" we might have brought back.

Gary, as I'll call him, came to Rogers to deal with a severe panic disorder. A divorced father with two daughters, Gary had battled his mysterious illness on and off for nearly two decades. For a ten-year period he had been on a medication which had kept him symptom free, but his body had grown used to it over time and it had suddenly become ineffective. It was difficult for Gary to pinpoint the cause of his extreme anxiety, as his panic attacks were never triggered by environmental factors or disturbing events. Just out of the blue he could be overwhelmed by a blinding terror, a fear so awful he would feel the urge to tear off all his clothes and run down the street screaming hysterically.

Last, but certainly not the least, Mitchell, as I will call him, had also traveled a long distance to Wisconsin for his treatment at Rogers. Along with having severe OCD, Mitchell had also recently struggled with substance abuse. Much like Betty, Mitchell often wasn't able to hide his symptoms from the view (or hearing) of others. Suffering from obsessions centered on his eyes, ears, and nose, Mitchell would frequently lock himself in the bathroom and blow his nose for hours at a time. It was the hardest and loudest I had ever heard anyone blow their nose! Unfortunately for Mitchell, this was an almost daily occurrence. His only relief during these dreadful episodes would be when he'd briefly stop to cuss loudly in frustration, or to dab away the blood dripping from his nose. On one occasion we heard him screaming and sobbing uncontrollably in the bathroom, even refusing staff requests to open the door. On several occasions, the OCD staff considered transferring Mitchell back to the main hospital building, all to protect the man from himself and his agonizing rituals.

While I naturally grew quite close to my housemates, it was also difficult to be around them 24-7, especially with regards to Betty and Mitchell. Seeing the two of them struggle through their daily symptoms was extremely traumatic for me. With having OCD, one gets so accustomed to the brutal nature of his/her own suffering that it's easy to take it for granted. To have to sit and watch another person go through it brings your strongest emotions to surface. Their struggles forced me to continuously face the reality of where I was and why I was here, and made me question whether the program was really any good. Though Gary was lucky enough, in our minds, to not have any rituals, ironically he in turn wished there was more he could do to reduce his tremendous distress. "I wish that I had rituals like you lucky OCD folks," he would often remark with a playful smile at the corner of his lips. With a more serious tone, he also voiced his genuine concerns about developing OCD. "I feel like I'm a step or two away from having OCD," he would often say. "If there was anything (rituals) I could do to reduce my anxiety, you just bet I would do it!"

Reducing anxiety is not what the program at Rogers is all about. On the contrary, the staff in the OCD program wants to make you feel anxious – extremely anxious – and have you sit with that anxiety until it slowly fades with the passage of time. To me, it was like they were saying that the only way to escape from the fire is by walking right through the flames! It seemed an unbearable torture, like there just HAD TO BE AN EASIER WAY to beat this disease. That's why I had traveled here to what I considered to be the "Promised Land", to finally discover the magical secret to defeating the illness. To be even more honest with myself, I was also hoping to be cared for and pampered a little; to gently be given the meds and treatment that would provide me the cure I so richly deserved. To learn that I'd now have to suffer even more was a truth that I couldn't yet face. However, it would soon become painfully clear to me that the true secret to defeating OCD is accepting THERE IS NO SECRET; that there's no way to really succeed without finally facing the things you most dread.

With the concept of facing one's worst fears being so daunting, the program at Rogers aims at accomplishing this goal by taking small steps. To do so, they use a scale to measure a person's anxiety level ranging from 0 to 7. While zero means no anxiety, levels one, two, and three represent a low amount of discomfort. Levels four, five, and six represent a significantly higher level of anxiety, while level seven stands alone as being the highest, most awful, unbearable level of distress one can feel. In order to not overwhelm new patients, the staff puts together a hierarchy of all your obsessive concerns, starting with having you confront your level three fears using the basic principals of cognitive behavioral therapy (CBT) as well as ERP, also called Exposure-Ritual Prevention. Just as it is written, ERP involves exposing yourself to what you're afraid of without carrying out the rituals that typically follow. Therefore, the method requires you to resist ritualizing – at least until your anxiety has gone down by one or two levels.

After creating your hierarchy, the staff assigns exposures for you to carry out on your own. Armed with a timer and a sheet of paper, you're expected to expose yourself to the particular fear and see how long it takes for your anxiety to drop a level or two (meaning if you started out at a three, you must continue exposure until discomfort goes down to a two or one.) At that point, you note how many minutes it took for the discomfort to reduce. The idea behind this strategy is the belief that over time, you will notice your level three fears changing to level ones, and that eventually you will find similar success with your level four and above fears as well.

In developing my hierarchy, it was difficult for me to identify those that would qualify as being my level three fears. After several meetings with David, the hierarchy specialist, we came up with several exposures for me to begin working on. They consisted of the following:

write the word "murder" repeatedly on a notepad
look at pictures of bullies from my past
discard a paper clip in garbage can with sharp point sticking out
hold plastic knife
hold DSM (Diagnostic Statistical Manual) but don't read
hold pair of worn underwear and don't wash hands

Although my main fears were obviously about harming or killing others, I had also mentioned to David my comparatively minor concerns about germs and contamination. Therefore, he felt it necessary for me to confront this part of my illness as well. Ironically, that turned out to be more of an unwanted exposure for my housemate Betty, who just about freaked out when she saw me parading around Lake House 3 holding a pair of worn underwear! Though we laughed about it at the time, she made darn sure to keep away from me for at least a good week. Soon it became a big joke between us, with her always refusing to bump into me as one of her assigned exposures. After a lot of pleading on my part (and urging from the staff), she reluctantly agreed to bump into me as well. Strange as it may seem, I felt honored to have been included! From that point on, I did the underwear bit in the privacy of my own room.

Along with our assigned exposures, the staff had each of us carry around a little bans book, listing all the different things we were banned from doing during treatment. For many of us these consisted of behaviors such as explaining ourselves too much or asking others for reassurance, along with checking, washing hands, and ritualizing. Challenging as they were, it was the explaining and reassurance bans that bothered me the most. All my life I've been a big time explainer, but as Karen, my behavior therapist told me, "We are very selective with whom we assign a ban for explaining themselves. So, if that is one of your bans, it is there because we feel you really need it." Not being able to ask for reassurance seemed even more cruel and unusual to me!

As it turned out, following the program itself proved to be the most difficult task I encountered at Rogers. With all the pressures and doubts about whether or not I would succeed, my OCD symptoms had reached an all time high. In fact, I was so overwhelmed with "unassigned" exposures that I was unable to complete the ones I was assigned! Almost every move I made was accompanied by the image of a bully, a ferocious threat about harming someone, or most often a mixture of both. The fact that I was not well medicated didn't help matters at all. Although Dr. Russell, the hospital's psychiatrist, had taken me off Seroquel and switched me to Anafranil (aka Clomipramine, to be taken along with Zoloft - a decision that would later produce amazing results), it would still be a dozen more weeks before the new meds would really kick in.

The staff at Rogers was, for the most part, extremely helpful through this very difficult time. Many of the RCs were young students close to me in age, and therefore easy for me to relate to. I will never forget some of the things they said and the advice they gave us. "OCD may manipulate you in countless ways, but it cannot make you violate your core values," was a statement made to me that I'll remember for the rest of my life. I was very impressed at the high level of understanding they all seemed to have about this complicated disease.

For example, I can never forget Cindy, a young woman with a big heart who literally helped me get into bed. I was struggling exceptionally hard one night in particular, and refused to leave Lake House 4 before completing a certain ritual. It was kind of funny in retrospect, as my intended ritual involved touching the inside of the bathroom door in Lake House 4. As it turned out, we had to wait there at least a half hour past the end of Cindy's shift for the bathroom to become available. The humorous twist was the fact that the person inside, a Lake House 4 resident, was struggling with her own rituals. "How sad is this?," I said to Cindy, trying to poke fun at the somber situation. "This poor girl can't get out of the bathroom and I just can't get in!" Already well past her shift, Cindy stayed with me until I could ritualize and then walked me back to my room. Once there, she was sweet enough to grab me some muffins from the kitchen since I was afraid of getting stuck into something if I were to get them myself.

Right along with all the good, there were those on the staff who seemed to take pleasure in poking and prodding us patients. At least that is how it felt at the time. Although I honestly believe they all had the best of intentions, it was their aggressive, confrontational style that some of us patients didn't like. We often felt scolded, as if we were poorly behaved children, almost blamed for not doing better with our difficult exposures. However, in retrospect, I can now see how difficult it can be for even the best of professionals to draw a clear line and distinguish when necessary pressure on highly resistant patients may become excessive and counterproductive.

It is also just as important to note that on the flip side, I had encountered a former fellow Rogers' patient in my OCD support group in Minnesota, who had successfully completed the residential treatment program in Oconomowoc. In contrast to how some residents and I had sometimes felt about the program, this young man had told me how much he had benefited from the hospital's tougher approach. "When I left Rogers at the end of my program, I personally thanked my lead therapist for being such a hard ass with me!" I recall this individual saying during a session with my OCD therapy group. In retrospect, I now believe that I would have likely done better myself at Rogers once my new meds had ample time to fully kick in; which, as it turned out did not occur until three months later, in July 2005. Given my status at the time of not being well medicated, along with my history of being bullied by people, I struggled to cope with this tougher approach.

Two weeks into my stay at Rogers, I seriously thought about leaving. The exposures I was assigned to do didn't seem to be very effective, and I felt isolated being the only resident there with the graphic harming obsessions. At any rate, I had finally run out of patience. After 16 hard days in Oconomowoc, I decided it was time to go home.

Ironically, many months would pass before I'd appreciate the benefit of making this difficult trip. After all, I certainly didn't walk out of that place a new and cured man! However, the change in my meds and the knowledge I had gained would slowly show their purpose over time.

As I packed my stuff to leave, I was visited in my room by Karen, the one behavior therapist who I felt had been the toughest on me. Rather than take advantage of this opportune moment to scold me, she instead expressed genuine regret that things hadn't gone very well for me during my shortened stay. "Good luck, too, with that book you're writing," she surprised me by saying with a smile. "Just keep working at it and I'm sure it'll turn out great!" With a rarely felt sense of confidence, I promised her that I would.

MY TIPS FOR POTENTIAL FUTURE PATIENTS TO SUCCESSFULLY COMPLETE THE OCD TREATMENT PROGRAM AT ROGERS:

While the staff at Rogers is very educated, helpful, supportive, and encouraging, do not rely on their efforts alone to "program" you. In spite of how talented they are, the staff cannot do the job for you or make your program succeed. Ultimately, your success in the program at Rogers will involve your finally having to face your tough fears and embrace the same old awful discomfort you have put so much of your time and energy into avoiding... at all costs. In my case, I went to Rogers fully believing that I would be taught some great, almost magical method which I could use to defeat my illness, and that I would be pampered by the staff after all of my difficult years. In reality, you will continue to use the same skills you learn at Rogers on your own in your personal home environment long after you've discharged. Do not rely on staff to coddle, protect, or enable you to continue to avoid facing your fears as other people in your life may have done in the past. There is no magical secret to the program or any easier, shortcut method to defeat OCD besides facing those same old ugly fears you've avoided now for ages. However, Rogers will provide you the unique opportunity to do so by following their proven approach, which will likely be a new experience for you. Do not feel intimidated or overwhelmed by this prospect when entering Rogers, but also remind yourself that this will require hard work on your behalf and a willingness to step outside of your usual comfort zone and face anxiety.

Cooperating with the resident psychiatrist and being open to possible changes in your medication regimen can provide immeasurable assistance in your battle with OCD. No one at Rogers can or will force you to do something you are not comfortable with. However, you must also remain willing to step outside of your usual comfort zone and at least try something different as recommended by the resident psychiatrist during your stay. In my case, being put on Anafranil by the psychiatrist at Rogers proved to be incredibly helpful for me in the long run!

You will encounter and be in close contact with other individuals who are also suffering with various forms of OCD while at Rogers. While you may likely grow close to your roommates and naturally feel sympathy towards them, it is helpful to not let such feelings consume you or begin to affect your personal program. It is also helpful to not compare your own progress, or lack thereof, with that of your fellow patients around you at Rogers. You should be prepared to see individuals who may appear to be doing better than you, as well as those individuals who may appear to be having a much harder time. Try to remain focused on yourself and to not be either encouraged or discouraged by the plights of the patients around you. In my case, I felt traumatized by seeing my fellow residents struggling hard with their OCD symptoms. Unlike you, I was not emotionally prepared in advance for this unavoidable aspect of daily life at Rogers. I also worried that if the program did not *appear* to be helping these other people, then perhaps it may also not work out for me. This negative, fearful mindset only caused me additional stress and served to discourage me prematurely. Remember, there are always hidden factors at play that you will not be aware of, which affect each individual patient's ability to endure their specific program while at Rogers. It is okay to be friends with your roommates, but keep your emotions in check and remember that you are there for yourself and for your own program. In this unique treatment environment and lifetime endeavor, it is OKAY to be selfish and to stay focused on YOU. There are trained professionals present 24/7 to assist your fellow patients, and you are not a bad or insensitive person for staying focused on yourself!

You may find that many people at Rogers will be focused on experiencing significant success *before* they leave this residential program and return to their home environments. While success is the overall goal and desired outcome of one's stay at Rogers, do not feel discouraged if you do not walk out of there feeling like a new man or woman upon your discharge. In my case, I put a tremendous amount of pressure on myself to be 'cured' and to ensure that I would walk out the doors as a brand new man. I feared that if I didn't experience significant success during my time at Rogers, there might be little hope for me to do so once I've finally been discharged. Again, this self-imposed pressure only served to discourage me and motivated me to leave Rogers after just 16 days. Recovery is not a perfect process, and in my case I did not experience significant success until three months *after* I had left Rogers! You may also be under the impression that your family, friends, and loved ones will be let down if you do not walk out of there as a highly changed person. Hopefully, those closest to you will be open to understanding that recovery from OCD is highly imperfect, and that their continued support will remain most beneficial to you in any event. If you by chance do not have this understanding or support from those closest to you, it will still help greatly for you to KNOW IT AND BELIEVE IT FOR YOURSELF. Please remember that I, for one, am a living example of this and will always believe in your resilient ability, as a unique individual, to slowly get better over time. That is how I did it and I know you can, too!

CHAPTER FOURTEEN
FINALLY FACING
MY FEARS

"The best way to handle an OCD fear is to face it, embrace it, and let time erase it."

As we all know by now, OCD is like an evil magician with a hat full of wicked tricks. Perhaps its greatest illusion is making us feel that we don't have any control. Like most seasoned abusers, OCD achieves this goal by use of threats and manipulation. Over time, we find ourselves being brainwashed into changing the way that we think. Slowly, we stray away from what we know is logical and true and embrace a whole bunch of irrational beliefs. The longer we follow this strange set of rules, the more we believe they are valid and real.

Though we may not realize it, the best way to free ourselves and regain control is to simply reverse this process. Just as everyone with OCD was brainwashed at some point, we are also fully capable of REPROGRAMMING HOW WE THINK! Having learned after Oconomowoc that there really is no quick fix, I began to try to reprogram my mind... or at least somebody else did.

Upon returning home from Wisconsin, my life hadn't changed that much. My days were still filled with rituals and worries still plagued my mind. Fortunately, my new girlfriend, the mother of the boy I'd been mentoring, took it upon herself to pick up a book that was collecting dust on my shelf. The book, called "Obsessive Compulsive Disorders: A Complete Guide To Getting Well and Staying Well" by Fred Penzel, PhD. had a section with reminders of why it was imperative to challenge the things that you fear. On her own initiative, my girlfriend wrote each of these key reminders on a small sheet of paper (like flashcards) and taped them all over my house! Whether I was sitting at the computer, putting food in the microwave, or even using the toilet, I was reading the notes she had written several times throughout each day. In this way, she hoped, those ideas would continually be reinforced in my mind. In July 2005, it finally started to work.

A LIFE INTERUPTED

It is important to note there was another major force that greatly helped in bringing about this change: It was the fact that I had chosen wisely this time to continue to take my new meds! Having been on medication now for over eight years, I had never really felt it working for me the way some patients described. Yes, doses of Risperdol and Seroquel (taken along with Zoloft) had helped me throughout the years, but I'd never felt that exhilarating boost certain patients said they received.

Never, that is, until July 2005, when I felt the motivation to attack my OCD! Back in April, Dr. Russell had started me on low doses of Anafranil, to be taken along with Zoloft and slowly increased with time. Anafranil, also called Clomipramine, is known as the oldest and perhaps the best drug for treatment of OCD. Dr. Russell had made this clear to me when prescribing it in Wisconsin. If this was true, I wondered, then why hadn't my doctor in Minnesota ever put me on this medication???

As I soon learned, Anafranil can also have side effects such as dry mouth, fatigue, and significant stomach troubles. Apparently, many patients are so bothered by the strong side effects that some doctors decline to prescribe it! Side effects I've experienced with Anafranil include increased fatigue, dizziness, and headaches. In other words, I tire more easily and can no longer go on most amusement park rides. Weight gain has been another side effect for me. I've also experienced increased sensitivity to temperature changes and physical exertion. In addition to these, I, too, have had some stomach problems and at times pass a lot of gas, although that particular side effect is more troubling to the people around me! Seriously speaking, however, it's a pretty small price to pay. The positive effects of Anafranil in my case really outweigh the bad.

This did not, however, mean that the medication would help me alone. While it corrected the chemical imbalance in my brain and leveled the playing field, there was still a very tough battle ahead. I like to use the analogy of the good old boxing fight to describe this scenario. Without the right meds, it was like I was fighting a much better boxer with a blindfold over my eyes and my hands tied behind my back. In other words, I didn't have a snowball's chance in hell of beating my opponent. With Anafranil, my eyes and hands are no longer bound and I feel a step ahead of my foe. Still, I cannot merely stand there and expect to win this difficult fight. I would now have to use the tough Exposure-Ritual Prevention approach I had learned at Rogers and really put it into practice. In the boxing match context, I'd have to throw some excellent punches, keep pace with my worthy opponent, and endure a whole bunch of very hard knocks.

This analogy almost literally applied with the first exposure I tried. Ever since the dreadful bunny incident in March, I had been most fearful of losing control and hitting someone I loved. Using our own interpretation of what I had learned at Rogers about Exposure Ritual Prevention, my girlfriend and I decided that my exposure would be for me to physically 'hit' her! Obviously this experiment would not involve actually harming my girlfriend, although in my mind I feared that it might. Rather, it would consist of confronting the irrational fear in a ballsy way that I had never attempted.

Regardless, the very first time we tried this it was TERRIFYING to me! It was surreal to see and feel my own hand slapping my girlfriend's cheek. As I continued to gently strike her on the side of her face, I feared that I'd become an abuser. Shockingly her reaction was quite different from mine. In fact, I couldn't have been more relieved when she laughed at my mock assault. "Oh come on now, you wimp, is that the hardest you can hit?" she managed to say between chuckles. I was astounded. Here I feared I'd become a batterer while she could barely conceal her amusement. I can honestly say that being made fun of had never felt so damn good!

Still shaking with fear, I forced my hand to continue gently striking her face. Along with laughing, she in turn began to playfully strike me back! It is important to note that we did this in the absence of her young son, who along with her had been physically abused by her ex-husband who was also the boy's father. In spite of our little experiment, my girlfriend insisted that I HADN'T abused her. Even though it would have been better to have not gotten this reassurance, it helped to know that she still saw me as the opposite of her son's dad.

Armed with this new confidence, I went on to repeat this and other tough exposures. One time, while watching TV with my girlfriend, I had an obsessive thought that I might hit her on her head with the remote control. On the spot, we decided to do an exposure where I gently 'struck' her head with the remote. As I cautiously bounced the small device on the top of her head, she couldn't help but laugh again at the absurdity of my actions. "You're the worst attacker in the world!" she said to me with laughter, even though I had requested her not to reassure me. In truth, I was relieved once again to know that I hadn't harmed her. Even though this exposure wasn't done with perfection, I'd begun to achieve my objective.

Encouraged by my own efforts, I made sure to keep track of my progress with these daring new exposures. The following are several major, major battles I fought in the war to regain my freedom from OCD. These began in July of 2005 and continued into the year 2006:

Biggest Challenges

- fear of throwing cell phone hard at Dad's face if I didn't bounce it again on car floor / suffered intensely but resisted for a whole day and the following day the anxiety slowly faded away / feared consequence did not happen... HUGE SUCCESS!!!

- fear of killing girlfriend's son if I didn't return to restroom in Wal-Mart and pick up tissue I had thrown in garbage can and instead flush it down the toilet / anxiety felt unbearable and I ended up ritualizing; feared consequence did not happen

- fear of hitting girlfriend's son on head if I didn't go back into Wal-Mart restroom and put hand under air-dryer / suffered extreme anxiety that evening but resisted and anxiety slowly faded away/ feared consequence did not happen

- fear of killing people if I didn't make sure if I possibly saw a piece of popcorn in popcorn bag / suffered extreme panic and anxiety right before falling asleep, felt "totally convinced" threat was real but feeling faded in the morning and over following two days / feared consequence did not happen

- fear of hitting girlfriend on head hard if I didn't delete part of chapter and then turn light on and off in bathroom / suffered what felt like unbearable anxiety and eventually ritualized; feared consequence did not happen

- fear of bouncing cell phone on a friend's and her baby's heads if I didn't re-write something on computer file first while sitting at computer with cell phone and glass of milk near / suffered what felt like unbearable anxiety, experiencing the feeling like I *absolutely had* to do the ritual or else... felt convinced more than ever that threat is real and I absolutely have to ritualize / feeling finally began to fade after a couple days of not ritualizing and continued to fade even more with next passing day / feared consequence did not happen... HUGE SUCCESS!!!

- fear of hitting Dad hard on back of head if I didn't re-touch my toes and be "sure" of exactly when my fingers left my toes / felt very strong anxiety at first, felt sure feared consequence was real, resisted ritualizing and faded quite quickly / feared consequence did not happen

- fear of hitting or killing people if I didn't rub cell phone against pillow a 2nd time when getting out of bed / feeling was very strong but faded quickly with good mood and attitude and not ritualizing / feared consequence did not happen

- fear of bumping my face into girlfriend's face while kissing her if I were to throw tissue in garbage can instead of down the toilet; feeling was absolutely unbearable, felt convinced that threat of harm was real/feared consequence did not happen; then also fear of dropping "WrestleMania ten" tape on girlfriend's head if I didn't go back and replay certain part of the tape; like previous one, the feeling was absolutely unbearable, felt convinced threat of harm was real; ritualized on both the following day after resisting all night and having dreams about doing the rituals; obsessive fears only worsened more and more as I ritualized; fear of hitting people on head with cell phone if I didn't walk downstairs with phone in my hand in a certain way, etc. Feared consequence did not happen

- fear of hitting girlfriend's son with left sandal if I didn't take it off left foot and put it back on in family room; feeling was unbearable all day long; felt beyond absolutely, absolutely convinced that threat or harm was real; finally ritualized during the evening; feared consequence did not happen

- fear of hitting girlfriend on head if I didn't have her re-pick up and move a bag of chips before watching the WrestleMania tape... image of Geraldo attached to it; then also fear of hitting someone on the head if I didn't scratch at little piece of skin on my thumb and imagine image of Geraldo over bully; tried to ritualize with second obsession but stopped short of satisfaction...; feeling was absolutely, absolutely unbearable... far beyond convinced that threat was real / fear faded; feared consequence did not happen

- fear of hitting, throwing something, or hurting someone if I didn't delete and re-write last fear item; felt extremely real / resisted and fear faded; feared consequence did not happen

- fear while watching a movie that I would have to hit someone on the head if I didn't re-watch certain scene and picture image of Geraldo in woman instead of bully's image; threat felt extremely real, felt completely convinced it would happen; after resisting for several days fear slowly melted away; feared consequence did not happen... HUGE SUCCESS!!!

- fear while watching a movie that I would for sure hit someone hard on the head or face if I didn't retouch something or move hand in a certain way; threat felt very, very strong but resisted and fear faded / feared consequence did not happen... HUGE SUCCESS!!!

- fear when playfully daring girlfriend to open car door while driving, fear of how far I'd actually go... *ritualized* later when lying on floor to sleep; feared consequence did not happen

- fear of hitting someone when waking up if I didn't rest head on corner of pillow... felt extremely real but resisted all day and feeling went down / feared consequence did not happen

- fear of harming someone if I didn't put computer cursor on certain square with arrow... had extreme doubt about whether or not it was real and that doubt made me feel like I could not take a chance... ritualized but not for long; feared consequence did not happen

- began ritualizing after making girlfriend's son's wrestlers hit one another, bumped my head against girlfriend's son as he slept, fell back into rituals but then confronted it by doing exposures... again bumping head into girlfriend's son's head, slapping girlfriend and Dad in the face; feared consequence did not happen

- fear of slapping Dad hard on the face/head... fear faded with time/feared consequence did not happen

- fear of losing control if I don't masturbate again and get out bully's image... fear faded with time... feared consequence did not happen

- DID A LOT OF RITUALIZING AND RUNNING FROM FEARS, TOO NUMEROUS TO NOTE DOWN; FEARED CONSEQUENCES DID NOT HAPPEN

- fear of hitting girlfriend on head if I didn't drop cell phone under seat in car... feeling began to fade but quickly grew stronger as new thoughts came in... then began to fade again but came back a few days later... became sooooooooooo incredibly powerful it felt like a panic attack... RITUALIZED TO EXHAUSTION UNTIL INTERRUPTED BY PHONE CALL/ feared consequence did not happen

- fear of hitting girlfriend if I didn't rewrite a new entry on "Lost Years" file (Images of a child I know)... feelings changed and feared both increased and decreased and increased... etc./ritualized to exhaustion, ultimately leading to banging my head against corner of table/feared consequence did not happen

- fear of dropping remote control on girlfriend's head and/or hitting her if I didn't retouch my hand to a part of car... some images of a child I know... felt 100 percent absolutely convinced that this one was different from all the rest and was for real.../ritualized once and then became preoccupied with desire to ritualize on previous item above/feared consequence did not happen

- fear of throwing cell phone in the air and having it land on someone hard if I didn't ritualize again on previous item above/faded with time, feared consequence did not happen

- fear of "losing control" and banging my head repeatedly on table corner again/ fear of eventually someday banging it harder than last night if I didn't give in and banged it then/faded with time, feared consequence did not happen

- fear of doubting, for even a second, that I might stab myself in the finger with fork at parents' house, if I didn't first do ritual with touching fork/salad bowl before writing anything in any of my files; feared consequences did not happen

As you can see from these notes, my battles were incredibly difficult and not always successful. But as time continued to pass I felt that something important had changed: IT WAS EASIER TO FACE MY OBSESSIVE CONCERNS, TO LIVE WITH DISCOMFORT, AND TO NOT RITUALIZE!!! From these experiences I soon came to learn that with each ritual I chose to perform, I was setting myself one small step away from recovery. This is so because every time I ritualized, I was programming my brain to believe that the threat that had led me to do so was real. This programming appeared to be automatic and involuntary, not something that I could consciously control, and it was through doing this countless times a day for over thirteen years that I had come to rely on rituals to dissipate OCD threats.

The good news, however, is that this negative effect can change with time if you simply apply the reverse. By not ritualizing and facing my fear until it slowly faded away, I was programming my brain to understand that the obsessive threats were *not* real! Simply put, not taking preventive action (ritualizing) sent a message to my brain that the perceived threat was nonsense and should be ignored. By repeating this basic process time and again, it got easier not to ritualize and to tolerate more distress. In other words, the "hard ass" approach I had learned at Rogers now seemed to be bearing fruit!

My exposures also brought other useful insights to my attention. Through the years, fear of hurting others had been the most awful obsessive concern for me. However, from reviewing my notes, I began to see that these feared consequences never really occurred. This observation helped me to realize that in spite of what OCD told me, I was *always* the one in control!

Strange as it may sound, this was quite a revelation to me. For years I had worried that because OCD got me to ritualize, perhaps it could also make me carry out other unwanted acts against my will. Ironically, those initial unwanted acts (rituals) only served to prove that I would go to endless lengths to prevent perceived harm from occurring! At any rate, my notes showed that whether I ended up ritualizing in a particular instance or facing my irrational fears, EITHER WAY I DIDN'T HARM ANYONE AS THE OCD THREATENED I WOULD!!! This served as powerful evidence that the OCD threats were not real. Rather, it seemed that they only had power and life if I chose to believe they were true.

As I began the year in 2006, I felt I'd regained control of my life. In fact, there were many great days where I recall feeling almost 100 percent symptom free! While this peacefulness lasted for several months, I knew it wouldn't stay forever. OCD tends to wax and wane in its nature, and can change over time like the weather. I've noticed that after doing well for some time, my symptoms often slowly try to creep back. By now I have come to realize that this common pattern should not be unexpected. The simple truth is that one can naturally get spoiled and forget how to face their difficult fears after having a lot of good times. Therefore, the sudden re-emergence of OCD symptoms can initially cause an individual doubts about the genuine progress they have made. "Oh my God, what did I do to bring this illness back into my life?! Where did I go wrong?! How can I handle these symptoms back in my life today?! Can I find my way through this stuff again?! Will it truly defeat me this time around?!" are all common initial reactions to the re-emergence of OCD. While this pattern may indeed continue, I now can choose and control how I handle my troubling symptoms. I can remind myself of the importance in choosing to welcome anxiety, which presents itself as being unwelcome, and in deciding to face my OCD fears instead of trying to ritualize them away.

As I write this paragraph at the end of 2007, I feel I have between 70-80 percent control of my OCD. This is quite a significant change from when I went to Rogers in April 2005, at which point I felt I had between 0-10 percent control of my illness. Lately I've been struggling with the age-old issue of trusting my basic perceptions. Once again, recent ritualizing appears to have deepened the nasty hole I have dug for myself, but today I understand what I'm up against and I know that it can't keep me down.

The story of my battle with OCD is no longer one of a life interrupted!

CHAPTER FIFTEEN

SUMMARY STATEMENT: TO MY FELLOW OCDERS WHO ARE STRUGGLING HARD WITH THEIR ILLNESS TODAY

I am writing this summary statement in mid-September 2010, now at the age of 34. As I do so, I'm delighted and grateful to say that I feel worlds apart from those most awful years when my illness consumed my existence. When my illness had been at its worst, I remember wishing for little other than to simply be free from that nearly continuous torment. I recall hearing others complain about seemingly trivial matters in their seemingly peaceful, privileged, OCD free lives, and I remember bitterly thinking of them as being horribly spoiled and ungrateful. Today, I'm well enough to often catch myself whining and complaining over that which, when I stop and really think about it, is also quite trivial in retrospect! At such moments, and also on a regular basis, I feel I have forgotten what it is like to have my life controlled by my illness. This, as opposed to fixating on an exact percentage of OCD-freeness, is perhaps the most accurate way for me to measure the progress that I have made.

At the very same time however, I am quick to point out that I STILL INDEED experience my numerous OCD symptoms on an almost daily basis (In fact shortly before writing the above mentioned positive statements about my progress, I found myself fearful that doing so may somehow trigger a brand new relapse!) I still experience images of bullies from my past and/or of persons I see as being evil, powerful, frightening, and intimidating. I still have strong obsessive fears about potentially harming others, about keeping others and myself safe from potential harm, and even about germs, contamination, and diseases. Given my utter fascination and interest in understanding violent crimes/criminals, I remain obsessive about home security and check my house (and sometimes my parents' home) for intruders on a regular basis.

Most difficult and frequent of all these, remain my doubts in not feeling able to trust my own basic perceptions (Did I just see a gray speck on the right corner of that sheet of paper? Did I just see a brown crumb in a certain part of my cereal bowl?, etc.). Not trusting perceptions also frequently includes when I walk through a crowded parking lot on a hot day, and then I suddenly doubt whether I just saw a helpless baby or animal – through a glass window - locked inside a sweltering car. This naturally happens most during the summertime, and in about half of such cases I make at least one attempt to double check and peek into the particular vehicle in question. It is the overall lack in severity/frequency of my symptoms in general today, due I believe to my painfully developed ability to reprogram my thinking and face more of my fears, which allows me to feel in control of my life and be able to enjoy things in life to the fullest.

It should go without saying that the leading reason for my continued success, I firmly believe, is my decision to faithfully take my prescribed medications. Ever since being switched to the medication Anafranil (aka Clomipramine) during my stay at Rogers Memorial Hospital in 2005, I feel I have dealt markedly better with my mental illness. As I write this summary statement in September 2010, I currently take 150 mg of Zoloft upon waking up and 75 mg of Anafranil in the few hours before going to sleep. I was initially put on 100 to 125 mg of Anafranil, but was able to lower the dosage to 75 mg over the years. I am also lucky to be able to report that the side effects from my meds - including weight gain, more fatigue, more passing gas, some headaches/dizziness, some loss of libido and vivid/unusual dreams while sleeping – are not overall significant enough to make me wish to change my current program.

It is also essential to mention that I've found recovery to be a highly imperfect process, consisting of difficult setbacks from time to time. In my case, I have often experienced a brief return of my worst OCD symptoms during times of physical tiredness, physical illness, and/or major emotional distress. Fortunately, after a couple of bad days, I have been able to quickly bounce back.

While I have laid out what I firmly believe to be a proven formula for success against OCD in this book, I realize that there are other factors at work that we may never be fully aware of. It is impossible to fully understand how and/or why some OCDers may experience success similar to mine or even better, while others who are every bit as deserving may have yet to get to that place.

This is why I especially wanted to reach out to my fellow OCDers who are struggling hard with their illness today. I want to tell you that I truly know how you are feeling and understand what you are living with on a day-to-day basis. If there was any way that I could get you to the better place where I am *finally* at today, please believe me that it would already be done. In spite of your ongoing hardships, I hope that my story can still provide you with hope and inspiration for your own progress in the near future. No matter how bad things may be for you right at this moment, I pray that you will never give up on yourself and your ability to someday, somehow get better. Regardless of how long you have been at the mercy of this crippling illness, please believe me when I say THERE CAN STILL BE LIFE AFTER OCD... and that your future can indeed be wonderful enough to see you through your hardships today. As long as a person remains alive, so, too, does the chance for change.

Last but not least my dear friend, from one true OCDer to another: Please think about my story in your darkest of moments and never give up on yourself.

ABOUT THE AUTHOR

Author and Speaker Sumi Mukherjee has two decades worth of painfully acquired expertise in dealing with bullying, anxiety, depression, and Obsessive-Compulsive Disorder. Since October of 2011, Sumi has been working on taking his message to hundreds of people around the country so others can benefit from his story. He is also working on completing two additional manuscripts to be published later in 2014. Sumi was born in Calgary, Canada, and grew up in Minnesota, USA.

Made in the USA
San Bernardino, CA
13 September 2015